THOMAS
REID

FAMOUS SCOTS SERIES

The following Volumes are now ready:—

THOMAS CARLYLE.   By HECTOR C. MACPHERSON.

ALLAN RAMSAY.   By OLIPHANT SMEATON.

HUGH MILLER.   By W. KEITH LEASK.

JOHN KNOX.   By A. TAYLOR INNES.

ROBERT BURNS.   By GABRIEL SETOUN.

THE BALLADISTS.   By JOHN GEDDIE.

RICHARD CAMERON.   By Professor HERKLESS.

SIR JAMES Y. SIMPSON.   By EVE BLANTYRE SIMPSON.

THOMAS CHALMERS.   By Professor W. GARDEN BLAIKIE.

JAMES BOSWELL.   By W. KEITH LEASK.

TOBIAS SMOLLETT.   By OLIPHANT SMEATON.

FLETCHER OF SALTOUN.   By G. W. T. OMOND.

THE BLACKWOOD GROUP.   By Sir GEORGE DOUGLAS.

NORMAN MACLEOD.   By JOHN WELLWOOD.

SIR WALTER SCOTT.   By Professor SAINTSBURY.

KIRKCALDY OF GRANGE.   By LOUIS A. BARBÉ.

ROBERT FERGUSSON.   By A. B. GROSART.

JAMES THOMSON.   By WILLIAM BAYNE.

MUNGO PARK.   By T. BANKS MACLACHLAN.

DAVID HUME.   By Professor CALDERWOOD.

THOMAS REID.   By Professor CAMPBELL FRASER.

THOMAS REID

BY A. CAMPBELL FRASER ::

FAMOUS SCOTS: SERIES

PUBLISHED BY
OLIPHANT ANDERSON
& FERRIER · EDINBVRGH
AND LONDON

The designs and ornaments of this volume are by Mr. Joseph Brown, and the printing from the press of Messrs. T. and A. Constable, Edinburgh.

PREFACE

This little book is an attempt to present Reid in a fresh light, and in his relations to present-day thought. It deals with the Scottish chapter in that enduring alternation between agnostic despair and endeavour after perfect insight which seems to be a law of the philosophic progress of mankind. Thomas Reid, home-bred and self-contained, is the national representative, in the eighteenth century, of the *via media* between these extremes. In the concluding chapter I have looked at the philosophical appeal to inspired data of Common Sense, in the wider light of the theistic philosophy of the universe, and not merely as part of an inductive science of the human mind. This connects the theistic postulate of spiritual reason, as the foundation of human experience, with Reid's appeal to the ultimate but often dormant necessities of human nature, a subject treated more fully in my *Philosophy of Theism* (1896).

For valuable unpublished material—more indeed than I could avail myself of within narrow limits—I am indebted to Miss Hilda Paterson, the guardian of manuscript remains and other relics of her ancestor, preserved at Birkwood, in Reid's native country of the Dee. I also owe much to Mr. R. S. Rait, now of New College, Oxford, the historian of the Universities of Aberdeen, whose research has done much to illustrate his *alma mater* in the North. And I am indebted to Dr. Davidson, the Professor of Logic, and to Mr. Anderson, the Librarian, of the University of Aberdeen, for documents to which the space at my disposal forbids more than an occasional reference.

Those who desire to study further the chapter in the history of European philosophy in which Reid's name is prominent, may be referred to Cousin's critical appreciation in his *Philosophie Écossaise* (1857), and to Professor Andrew Seth's Balfour Lectures on 'Scottish Philosophy' (1885), in which the Scottish and German answers to Hume are compared. The industry of the late Dr. M'Cosh has collected, in his *Scottish Philosophy* (1875), interesting particulars regarding our national philosophers from Hutcheson to Hamilton.

A. C. F.

UNIVERSITY OF EDINBURGH,
  21*st February* 1898.

CONTENTS

CHAPTER I

PAGE

BOYHOOD AND ANCESTRY: STRACHAN AND THE VALLEY OF THE DEE, 1710-1722 9

CHAPTER II

AT MARISCHAL COLLEGE, 1722-1737 18

CHAPTER III

NEW MACHAR AND DAVID HUME, 1737-1751 . . . 30

CHAPTER IV

OLD ABERDEEN: A REGENT IN KING'S COLLEGE, 1751-1764   43

CHAPTER V

UNIVERSAL SCEPTICISM VERSUS INSPIRED COMMON SENSE: AN 'INQUIRY INTO THE HUMAN MIND ON THE PRINCIPLES OF COMMON SENSE,' 1764 56

CHAPTER VI

GLASGOW COLLEGE: THE PROFESSOR OF MORAL PHILOSOPHY, 1764-1780 72

CONTENTS

CHAPTER VII

IN PHILOSOPHICAL RETIREMENT: AUTHORSHIP IN OLD AGE, 1780-1795 103

CHAPTER VIII

INSPIRED COMMON SENSE AND CAUSATION: ACTIVE OR MORAL POWER IN MAN 118

CHAPTER IX

THE END, 1796 126

CHAPTER X

RETROSPECTIVE AND CRITICAL 133

CHAPTER XI

REID IN THE NINETEENTH CENTURY: DEVELOPMENT OF THE COMMON SENSE PHILOSOPHY: REID IN FRANCE: REID AND HAMILTON: REID AND SCOTO-HEGELIAN IDEALISM: ETHICAL OR THEISTIC FINAL FAITH . . 144

THOMAS REID

CHAPTER I

BOYHOOD AND ANCESTRY: STRACHAN AND THE
VALLEY OF THE DEE

1710—1722

THOMAS REID makes his first appearance as a boy in the manse of Strachan in Kincardineshire, where he entered this world of sense on the 26th of April 1710. His father, the Rev. Lewis Reid, was minister of the parish for fifty-eight years, from 1704 until his death in 1762. The mother, Margaret Gregory, was the eldest daughter, by his second marriage, of David Gregory, laird of Kinairdy in Banffshire. An elder son, David, born in 1705, and two daughters, Isobel and Jane, with Thomas, formed the family at the manse when Thomas was a boy. David was twice married, and died about 1780, without issue; the elder daughter, Isobel, died unmarried, in her stepmother's house at Aberdeen, in 1770; and the younger, Jane, after a *mésalliance*, died without issue after the middle of the century. Their mother, Margaret Gregory, died in 1732, when the manse was still the home of Thomas. In 1735, Mr. Lewis Reid married his second wife, Janet, daughter of Fraser of Phopachy in the county of Inverness. Two sons and five daughters were the issue of the second marriage. The eldest son died when a student at Marischal College, in 1758, and the younger, who studied medicine, died in London about ten years later. Of the daughters, one died in infancy, and two others, Elizabeth and Mary, died unmarried—the former in Edinburgh in 1772, and the latter in Aberdeen in 1771. Of the other two, Margaret became in 1763 the wife of the Rev. Alexander Leslie, minister of Fordoun in Kincardineshire, and Grace married the Rev. John Rose, minister of Udny in Aberdeenshire. Mrs. Rose died in 1793, and Mrs. Leslie in 1829, the last survivor of the Reid family circle at Strachan.[1]

It is recorded of the father of this large family that he was respected for piety, prudence, and benevolence, inheriting from his ancestors simplicity of manners, and literary tastes which, without attracting the notice of the world, engaged his leisure and dignified his rural life. Of the two wives, the second survived her stepson, the philosopher.

The remote parish of Strachan is formed by the romantic valley through which the Feugh finds its way from the Grampians to the Dee at Banchory-Ternan—a breezy upland region, redolent of heather and bog-myrtle, apt in its solitude to educate reflective individuality in one so disposed. In those days the road to the south over the Cairn o' Mount passed through Glen Dye, under the shadow of Clochnaben, a road two centuries ago frequented by robbers, and invested with a halo of romance by tales of marvellous adventures. But Glen Dye has an interest of another kind. Centuries ago it was the home and property of the family of Cant, from whom Andrew Cant, the noted Covenanting preacher, was descended,[2] and

---

[1] The above from data at Birkwood.
[2] *Scottish Notes and Queries*, iii. 84-88; 128.

with whom the more widely celebrated Immanuel Kant, chief factor in the philosophical thought of modern Europe, claimed connection. Strachan is thus associated in imagination with two of the most illustrious thinkers of the eighteenth century. Thomas Reid is in this way connected locally with his famous German philosophical contemporary, as well as by parallels in their lives which appear in the sequel, and by spiritual analogies in their philosophy. They are moreover united by their common antagonism to the scepticism of David Hume, who also through them is associated with the moorland valley of the Feugh, making it suggest to fancy three memorable intellectual figures. In Scotland David Hume and Thomas Reid are the two greatest names of their century in philosophy.

Imagination is our only guide when we try to picture the boyhood of Thomas Reid in the homely surroundings at Strachan. The one recorded fact about him is, that in his tenth year the home education of the manse was followed by two years spent in the neighbouring parish school of Kincardine O'Neil. Thus far no signal signs of future eminence appeared. He was, it seems, an unprecocious youth, remarked for modesty and patient industry. The insight of the schoolmaster is said to have found in him the rudiments of a man of 'good and well-wearing parts.' I wish that some further record could be found of this sagacious prophet of his pupil's steady mental concentration, and I have not discovered why the boy was placed in the Kincardine school. This dim picture is our only one in the first twelve years of his life.

The lack of personal incident in those years is in a manner compensated by the interest of an illustrious ancestry—Reids and Gregories. He inherited mind through his father, but much more through his mother, with whom he shared the unique celebrity of a family which in successive generations shed lustre on the valley of the Dee—a memorable example of inherited intellect.

In the end of the fourteenth century certain lands of Pitfodels, between the bridge of Dee at Aberdeen and the Den of Cults, became the property of William Reid, a kinsman of the former owner, Alexander Moray, 'lord of Culboyne.' The lands remained in the Reid family until the beginning of the sixteenth century, when Marion, heiress of Alexander, the last Reid of Pitfodels, married Thomas, the eldest son of Gilbert Menzies, a burgess of Aberdeen, whose family was known thereafter for three centuries as Menzies of Pitfodels. James Reid, the first minister of Banchory-Ternan after the Reformation, was, it seems, grandson of a younger brother of this Alexander of Pitfodels; and Lewis Reid, the minister of Strachan, was in direct descent from the minister of Banchory. It is told of James Reid that he was 'a man of notable head-piece for witte, and the most of his children were men of extraordinary qualifications.' His eldest son, Robert, noted for good sense, succeeded him at Banchory. The second son, Thomas, was one of the numerous Scots famed for learning, who migrated to the Continent in the end of the fifteenth century and after. He was educated partly at Marischal College, Aberdeen, where he was made regent about 1602. He was afterwards in residence at Oxford and abroad: he defended a thesis '*De objecto Metaphysicæ*' at Rostock in 1610. After his return to Britain he became Greek and Latin Secretary to King James, some of whose works he translated into Latin. Verses of his may be found in the '*Delitiæ Poetarum Scotorum.*' Alexander, the next brother, was physician to Charles I., and author of works in physiology well considered at that time. John, a brother of the minister of Banchory, translated into 'the Scottishe tunge' Buchanan's *History of Scotland*, and this unpublished version is in the College of Glasgow. A second Robert, grandson of the eldest of these four sons, became minister of Banchory at the Restoration; he was a member of the first Episcopal Synod at Aberdeen in the restored Establishment (the Covenanting Alexander Cant was his immediate predecessor); he died in 1682. Thomas, the second son, 'wadsetter of Eslie in Banchorie,' was father of the Rev. Lewis Reid of Strachan, by his wife, Jane, a niece of Sir Thomas Burnett of Leys; and thus young Thomas Reid at Strachan was related to the family from which the historian Bishop Burnet was descended. These Reids of Banchory rest in the old burial-ground there, 'not farre from the banke of the river Dee, expecting the general resurrection, and the glorious appearing of Jesus Christ there Redemier.'

But the Gregory connection of Thomas Reid through his mother is, as I have said, more significant than the Reid succession. During the Civil Wars of the seventeenth century, the minister of the rural parish of Drumoak, on the north side of the Dee, between Banchory and Pitfodels, was the Rev. John Gregory, son of an Aberdeen merchant, whose father was a M'Gregor from Glenlyon. The Gregories of Deeside were thus descendants of the clan Gregor of Glenlyon and Glenstrae, a circumstance referred to by Sir Walter Scott in the Introduction to *Rob Roy*. The minister of Drumoak married a lady named Anderson, one of a family reputed for mathematical ability in successive generations. She inherited the genius of her family, and transmitted it to her sons. Her husband at Drumoak seems to have steered his cause skilfully in that troubled time, for he bought the good estate of Kinairdy, part of the heritage of the lordly house of Creighton Viscount Frendraught. Alexander, the eldest son of the Rev. John Gregory of Kinairdy, was killed by one of the Creightons in a fray in 1663, and the homicide was the occasion of a *cause célèbre*. David, the second son, succeeded his murdered brother in the lands of Kinairdy, and shared in the mathematical inheritance of the Gregories. For some reason he sold Kinairdy and became an energetic merchant, spending part of his life in Holland. This David of Kinairdy was twice married, and father of twenty-nine children, which perhaps explains the sale. The wife of the Rev. Lewis Reid of Strachan was a daughter of the second marriage. Three of her brothers were eminent Professors of Mathematics in British Universities—namely, David, first at Edinburgh, and then at Oxford, the friend of Newton; James, the successor of David in Edinburgh; and Charles, who professed mathematics at St. Andrews. David's son was Professor of History at Oxford from 1724 till 1767, and Dean of Christ Church; and his cousin David succeeded to the chair of Mathematics at St. Andrews. Two other Professors were sons of two of 'Kinairdy's' daughters—namely, our Thomas Reid, and Alexander Innes, who professed Philosophy in Marischal College. These all traced their birth to the minister of Drumoak and his mathematical wife—through their son David. But James, the third son of the Drumoak manse, was not less illustrious in himself and in his descendants. He was Professor of Mathematics, first at St. Andrews and then at Edinburgh, inventor of the reflecting telescope, also Newton's friend and correspondent, who introduced the science of Newton into the Universities of Scotland. It is of him that Whiston writes from Cambridge:—'He had already caused several of his students to keep acts upon several branches of the Newtonian philosophy; while we at Cambridge, poor wretches, were ignominiously studying the fictitious hypotheses of the Cartesian.' His son James became in 1725 Professor of Medicine in King's College, Aberdeen, a considerable local figure. He had two sons: James, who succeeded his father, and John, a regent of philosophy in his father's college, afterwards Professor of Medicine in Edinburgh, and remembered as the author of *A Comparative View of Man and the Animal World*, and *A Father's Legacy*, books full of good sense. Dr. John Gregory's son, James, was Professor of Medicine in Edinburgh from 1776 till 1821, a physician and a metaphysician —in the sequel, the intimate friend and correspondent of Thomas Reid, and the patron of Thomas Brown. Of his family, one son held the Chair of Chemistry in King's College, and afterwards in Edinburgh till his death in 1858; another, Donald, was an eminent archæologist, author of the *History of the Western Highlands and Islands*; a third died in high mathematical repute at Cambridge, returning to the original bent of this extraordinary family, in which the disposition to mathematics had latterly been overborne by medicine and moral philosophy. Even this long list of names omits scientific celebrities who were descended from the minister of Drumoak and his wife, Margaret Anderson, more remotely still from the wild clan Gregor of Glenlyon and Glenorchy.

But the life of romantic adventure did not descend to young Thomas Reid at Strachan. A disposition to look at the world on its moral and religious side, perhaps inherited from the Reids, with a strong bent to mathematics and the scientific side of things, inherited from the Gregories, along with his own patient, concentrated reflection, was the inheritance of the boy 'of good and well-wearing parts' who left the Kincardine school in 1722. The long life that followed presents none of the outward incidents that readily touch the popular fancy; but to those awake to the higher problems of human life it touches thought and imagination in another fashion. It has been said that a human life should resemble a well-ordered poem: the exordium should be simple and should promise little. This condition is fulfilled in the life of Thomas Reid, which, to the end, was modestly spent in learned retirement, indifferent to vulgar fame. Its chief interest lies in the spectacle of penetrating sagacity, independent and sincere, steadily devoted to the invisible world of thought and belief, in quest of the ultimate foundations and guarantees of human knowledge. It should attract those who, in an age of sceptical criticism, seek to assure themselves of the final trustworthiness of the experience into which, at birth, they were admitted as strangers, ignorant of what the whole means, like the agnostic in Pascal. Who has sent me into this life, I know not; what the world around me is, I know not; nor what I am myself. I find myself chained to one little planet, but without understanding why I am here rather than there; and why this period of time was given me to live in rather than any other in the unbeginning and endless duration. Life with its memories and forecasts looks like a blind venture. The sum of my knowledge seems to be that I must die; but what I am most ignorant of is the meaning of death. One is drawn to Reid by an interest in final questions like these, which the agnostic spirit is now forcing upon us. It was the sceptical disintegration of human knowledge and belief that was going on in his own time that led Reid, with the patience and persistency revealed in his boyhood, to devote a long life to testing in his own sincere fashion man's intellectual and moral footing in that world of sense which, all strange to it, he entered in the valley of the Feugh.

CHAPTER II

AT MARISCHAL COLLEGE

1722—1737

AT the age of twelve Reid emerges out of the obscurity in which his boyhood lies concealed from us. In one of his letters to his cousin, Dr. James Gregory, written in his old age, he mentions 'April 1722' as the date of his first visit to Aberdeen, then a town of some eight thousand inhabitants, and twenty miles distant from the moorland valley in which he was born. He tells how he was taken to see his grandmother, who was living in Aberdeen, the second wife and widow of David Gregory of Kinairdy. 'I found her,' he says, 'old and bedridden, but I never saw a more ladylike woman. I was now and then called into her room, when she sat upon her bed, or entertained me with sweetmeats and grave advices. Her daughters that assisted her often, as well as one who lived with her, treated her as if she had been of a superior rank; and indeed her appearance and manner commanded respect. She and all her children were zealous Presbyterians: the first wife's children were Tories and Episcopalians.' This picture of the boy in Aberdeen we owe to his movement from the country school in the valley of the Dee to the higher sphere of the Aberdeen Grammar School, which he seems to have entered in that April, encouraged perhaps by the prognostic of the

Kincardine schoolmaster. The Grammar School Register tells that in 'October 1722' Thomas Reid left it to enter Marischal College, where his name appears in the list of those matriculated that autumn. It was an early age for University life according to later ideas, but not at variance with the custom of Scotland in those days. Burnet, afterwards Bishop of Salisbury, another eminent Aberdonian, entered Marischal College when he was only nine, and graduated when he was thirteen; and Burnet's contemporary, Reid's granduncle, James Gregory, graduated when he was not older than Burnet.

The uncouth and dilapidated structure in which the University of the Earls Marischal was housed when young Reid was spending his undergraduate years in it, bore no resemblance to the stately College on the same site which now adorns the prosperous city of Bon Accord. The process of decay was so rapid, and the case was so urgent, that a few years later the regents suspended their official claim to a part of the scanty funds of the College, and also asked help from the community, 'to preserve from ruin an university from whence so many accomplished men have gone forth as ornaments of their country in every age since its foundation.' The troubles of 1715 had further reduced its resources. Its Chancellor, the tenth Earl Marischal, concerned in the rising of Mar, then forfeited his title and the official connection of his family with the academical foundation of his ancestor. The Principal and most of the authorities had been removed or suspended by a commission of visitation in 1717. During the two years which followed the adventure of Mar the doors of Marischal College were closed, so that, when public instruction was resumed in 1717, a new race of teachers was in possession, and, as it happened, an era of intellectual activity was inaugurated.

Notwithstanding the humble accommodation which it offered, and the social revolution through which it had lately passed, Marischal College could then boast of at least three eminent teachers, imbued with the spirit of the 'new philosophy,' and of the reviving literary taste in Scotland. The Professor of Mathematics was Colin M'Laurin, brother of the eloquent Presbyterian preacher, himself among the foremost of British mathematicians, a friend and correspondent of the aged Newton, who, along with Reid's inherited disposition, attracted the young student to the study in which the teacher was a master. And about the time when Reid entered College, Thomas Blackwell, a critic of Homer, and author of *Memoirs of the Court of Augustus*, prominent among his countrymen who were anxious to write good English, became Professor of Greek, and for a generation encouraged classical taste and love of literature in the north of Scotland. But the teacher who chiefly influenced Reid's undergraduate life was George Turnbull, a copious author, though his books are little remembered now. He was Reid's guide for three years; for the College was then under a system of 'regents' which intrusted the student to the same teacher in all the three years given to 'philosophy'—natural as well as moral.

Reid was fortunate in entering Marischal College when it was inspired by M'Laurin, Blackwell, and Turnbull, each a leader in the scientific and literary awakening of the time. The Aberdeen of 1725 was no longer the Aberdeen of the ministers of whom Gordon in his *Scots Affairs* tells that they shrieked, 'downe with learning and up with Christ.' Their religion was in alliance with culture and progressive intelligence, anticipating in the North the intellectual enlargement associated in the West with the University of Glasgow under Hutcheson, Leechman, and Adam Smith.

George Turnbull is little known now, but he is too important a factor in the making of Thomas Reid to be lightly passed over. He was an Edinburgh graduate, born in 1698, and like Reid a son of the manse. He became a regent of philosophy in Marischal College at the age of twenty-three. The College record informs us that on the 14th of April 1726 he presented for graduation a band of thirty-nine students: the name of Thomas Reid appears last in the list. Turnbull's lectures when he was regent were in 1740 embodied in his *Principles of Moral Philosophy*. His leading arguments are illustrated and vindicated by quotations from Berkeley's *Theory of Vision* and *Principles of Human Knowledge*, also by the *Inquiry* of Francis Hutcheson and the *Sermons* of Bishop Butler. The influence of Berkeley is evident.

The mottoes on the title-page of Turnbull's book express his method of inquiry. One of them is the precept of Pope—'Account for moral as for natural things'; the other expresses in the words of Newton the consequence which may be expected to follow—'If Natural Philosophy, in all its parts, by pursuing this method, shall at length be perfected, the bounds of Moral Philosophy will also be enlarged.' Turnbull was among the first in Scotland to substitute, in mental philosophy, tentative study of the facts of human nature for logical deduction from abstract dogmas. 'If a fact be actually found, either in the outer world of sensible things, or in the inner and invisible world of mind, there is no room for reasoning against it. Every reasoning, however subtle, if it be repugnant in its conclusion to the actual fact of the case, must be sophistical.' Turnbull is fond of repeating that facts presented to the senses are not the only, nor yet the most important, facts which the universe contains. The invisible facts which take the form of beliefs and feelings and volitions are the deepest facts of all: spirit and not matter at last regulates life. Then he refers to what he calls 'common sense' as the final arbiter in all questions. 'Common sense is sufficient to teach those who think of the matter with seriousness and attention all the duties of common life; all our obligations to God and our fellow-men; all that is morally fit and binding.' In a word, spiritual facts of mind are not to be crushed out of existence by tangible and visible facts of matter. That mind in the form of will is the only known active power is another prominent lesson in Turnbull's teaching. 'It is will alone that manifests power or productive energy. To speak of any other active power in the universe is to speak without meaning; because experience, the source of all the materials of our knowledge, does not lead us to any other conception of power.' Turnbull's conception of the material world is very like Berkeley's. Matter is the established or natural order in which sense ideas present themselves. 'Properly speaking, what we call matter and space are only sensible ideas, produced in us, according to an established or natural order, by some external cause; for when we speak of material things, we can only mean certain sensible perceptions that arise in our minds, according to a fixed order, but which are experienced to be absolutely inert or passive, having in themselves no productive force.' It was in this philosophy that Turnbull's most famous pupil was educated at Marischal College.

THOMAS REID

Turnbull's official connection with the College lasted only six years. After inaugurating moral philosophy in the modern spirit in Scotland, he resigned in the spring of 1727, and, after some residence abroad, lived in London, producing books in excess of the demand for them. He ended by taking orders in the Irish branch of the Anglican Church, finding the communion of Jeremy Taylor and Berkeley more suited to his temper than the fervid Presbyterianism to which he was accustomed in his youth. In search of health, he died at the Hague in 1749.

I have enlarged on Turnbull, because by him Reid was first attracted to the study of the human mind. But Blackwell, the Professor of Greek, must not be forgotten. Blackwell, as well as Turnbull, was connected with Berkeley. It was when Reid was at Marischal College that Berkeley was engaged in the most romantic missionary enterprise of that age, for spreading Christian civilisation in America by a College in the Bermudas. Curiously, Blackwell was one of those whom he asked to join the little party of missionaries who embarked with him at Gravesend in September 1728, after he had surrendered high preferment in Ireland in order to devote his life to a more cosmopolitan philanthropy. The Aberdeen regent was not prepared for the sacrifice. He refers thus to Berkeley's adventure:—

'In this respect I would with pleasure do justice to the memory of a very great though singular sort of man, known as a philosopher, and intended founder of a University in the Bermudas or Summer Islands. An inclination to carry me out with him on that expedition, as one of the young professors on his new foundation, having brought us often together, I scarce remember to have conversed with him on that art, liberal or mechanic, of which he knew not more than the ordinary practitioners. With the widest views, he descended to the most minute detail, and begrudged neither pains nor expense for the means of information. I enter not into his peculiarities, either religious or personal, but admire the extensive genius of the man, and think it a loss to the Western world that his noble and exalted plan of an American University was not carried into execution.'—*Memoirs of the Court of Augustus.*

The fact that Berkeley was so much in evidence at Marischal College in those days, through Turnbull and Blackwell, is significant of much in the life of Reid.

If Reid recorded his thoughts when he was a student at Marischal College, the record has been lost. A commonplace book like Berkeley's, when Berkeley was an undergraduate in Dublin, would have cast welcome light on this part of his mental history. The only extant revelation of his inner life in these years is contained in a letter written half a century after to his kinsman William Gregory at Oxford. It relates to the period when his year was divided between town and country—the winters at Aberdeen and the long summer days at the manse of Strachan :—

'About the age of fourteen I was,' he says, 'almost every night unhappy in my sleep from frightful dreams : sometimes hanging over a dreadful precipice, and just ready to drop down ; sometimes pursued for my life and stopped by a wall, or by a sudden loss of strength ; sometimes ready to be devoured by a wild beast. How long I was plagued with such dreams I do not recollect. I believe it was for a year or two at least ; and I think they had left me before I was fifteen. In those days I was much given to what Mr. Addison in one of his " Spectators " calls *castle-building*; and in my evening solitary walk (which was generally all the exercise I took), my thoughts would hurry me into some active scene, where I generally acquitted myself much to my own satisfaction, and in those scenes of imagination I performed many a gallant exploit. At the same time, in my dreams I found myself the most arrant coward. Not only my courage but my strength failed me in every danger ; and I often rose from my bed in the morning in such a panic that it took some time to get the better of it. I wished much to get free of these uneasy dreams, which not only made me unhappy in sleep, but left a disagreeable impression on my mind for some part of the following day. I thought it was worth trying whether it was possible to recollect while I was dreaming that it *was* all a dream, and that I was in no danger. Accordingly, I often went to sleep with my mind as strongly impressed as I could with this thought—that I never in my lifetime had been in any real danger, and that every fright I had was a dream. After many fruitless endeavours to recollect this when the danger appeared, I effected it at last, and have often, when I was sliding down a precipice into the abyss, recollected that it was all a dream, and boldly jumped down. The effect of this commonly was that I immediately awoke ; but I awoke calm and intrepid, which I thought a great acquisition. After this my dreams were never very uneasy ; and in a short time I dreamed not at all. During all this time I was in perfect health ; but whether my ceasing to dream was the effect of the recollection above mentioned, or of any change in the habit of my body, which is usual about that period of life, I cannot tell. I think it may more probably be imputed to the last. However, the fact was that for at least forty years after I dreamt none, to the best of my remembrance ; and finding from the testimony of others that this is somewhat uncommon, I have often as I awoke endeavoured to recollect, without being able to recollect anything that passed in my sleep. The only distinct dream I ever had since I was about sixteen, as far as I remember, was about two years ago (1777). I had got my head blistered for a fall. A plaster which was put upon it after the blister pained me excessively for a whole night. In the morning I slept a little, and dreamed very distinctly that I had fallen into the hands of a party of Indians and was scalped. I am apt to think that, as there is a state of sleep and a state wherein we are awake, so there is an intermediate state which partakes of the other two. I have slept on horseback, but so as to preserve my balance ; and if the horse stumbled, I could make the exertion necessary to save me from a fall, as if I was awake.'

In all this one detects the disposition to sober introspection, which ripened as life advanced.

During the ten years that followed the graduation in April 1726 we have only faint traces of Reid. In the following winter he began to study theology, and in 1731 he had completed the course required by the Church, under the direction of Professor James Chalmers, father of the founder of the *Aberdeen Journal*. This is another parallel between Reid and Kant: both, it seems, were theologically trained.

Reid's name first appears in the books of the Presbytery of Kincardine O'Neil when he was in his nineteenth year. Extracts from the minutes with which I have been favoured record his progress with a quaint simplicity not without interest, as part of the history of a philosopher:—

'On the 17th of July, 1728, James Lumsden, John Beaton, Thomas Reid, and David Ross, students in divinity, residing within the bounds of the presbytery, being now present, the presbytery thought fit to appoint each of them to be in readiness to deliver a homily against the next meeting, and accordingly appointed Mr. Reid to deliver a homily on John i. 29.—18 September 1728. This day Mr. Thomas Reid delivered his homily, with which the presbytery being satisfied, the moderator encouraged him to go on with his studies.—8th June 1731. The presbytery considering that Mr. Thomas Reid had been allowed by the Synod to enter upon tryal, and he, being upon the place, did undergo questioning tryal, wherein he was approved, and the presbytery appointed him to be in readyness to deliver a lecture on Ps. ii., and an exegesis on that common head. *Num detur peccatum originale inherens.*—22nd September 1731. This day Mr. Thomas Reid underwent a questioning tryal and was approved. And the presbytery taking into consideration that he, having passed his course in Arts at the College, and thereafter having studied Divinity for the space of   [1] years, as also having resided for the whole of this

[1] The number is, unfortunately, unrecorded.

PHILOSOPHICAL WORKS

By PROFESSOR CAMPBELL FRASER

The Collected Works of Bishop Berkeley. With Prefaces, Annotations, his Life, and a Critical Account of his Philosophy. 4 vols. 8vo. £2, 18s. (Clarendon Press.)

'At length we have a complete edition of Berkeley's Works, which reflects honour alike on the Oxford University Press and on the University of Edinburgh.'—*Edinburgh Review*.

The Essay concerning Human Understanding. By JOHN LOCKE. Annotated with Prolegomena, Biographical, Critical, and Historical. 2 vols. £1, 12s. (Clarendon Press.)

'An edition of the great Philosophical Classic of which the English-speaking world may well be proud.'—*American Philosophical Review*.

Philosophy of Theism. Gifford Lectures. 2 vols. 15s. (Blackwood and Sons.)

'The University of Edinburgh was well advised in appointing to its Gifford Lectureship the Editor of Berkeley and Locke. These two volumes, as a continuous piece of reasoning, form a notable and a very timely contribution to philosophical and religious thought.'—*Quarterly Review* (January 1898).

'These lectures form unquestionably one of the finest products of the Gifford Trust.'—*Athenæum*.

'These powerful lectures present a very striking exposition of the bases of natural theology in the widest sense of the term.'—*Times*.

'A work which must take a high place in the apologetic literature of this century. No more impressive *apologia* for religion has appeared in our time.'—*Guardian*.

time within the bounds of this presbytery; and they looking upon him as a person fit to be entered upon tryals, and also having had sufficient testimonials from the professors of divinity with whom he studied as to his proficiency in his studys and good behavour, he was admitted to the usual tryals appointed by the Acts of the General Assembly of this Church, and having passed through all the parts thereof, he was licensed by the said presbytery to preach the Gospel of Christ, and exercise his gifts as a probationer for the holy ministry.'

On the 2nd of August 1732, 'the Presbytery chose Mr. Thomas Reid to be their Clerk.' On the 5th of October in the same year, 'the Presbytery appointed Mr. Thomas Reid to supply at Lumphanan the second Sabbath after Mr. Gordon's removal.' On the 8th of November, 'Mr. Thomas Reid was continued Clerk till the next meeting of the provincial Synod,' in April 1733.

In July 1733 Reid re-appears, this time not engaged in ecclesiastical ministration, but as the librarian of Marischal College. It was an office with which he had a family connection. 'The most outstanding name in the history of Marischal College Library,' says Mr. Rait, 'is that of Thomas Reid, Latin secretary to James VI., son of James Reid, minister of Banchory-Ternan. In 1624 he left to Marischal College his own library, 6000 merks to be invested in land, and a sum of money to provide a salary for a librarian.' The secretary's brother, Alexander, also bequeathed books of philosophy and divinity. And David Gregory of Kinairdy was for some time librarian. It was an acceptable retreat for research, and a mark of esteem from the College. Mr. Rose, Reid's brother-in-law, says that he then studied Newton's *Principia* and Locke's *Essay*.[1] Again a parallel between Reid and Kant. Some

[1] Birkwood MSS.

time after Kant had taken his degree he was made librarian in the Schloss Library, with a yearly stipend of about £10. This was nominally in excess of Reid's modest honorarium of £9 at Aberdeen, a pittance which was for a time suspended by threatened litigation. He was in active service as librarian till 1736, and for two years more in possession, 'on leave of absence, with a substitute.'

The need for a 'substitute' in 1736 can be explained. In that year, for the first time, Reid is found outside Scotland. He is making a tour in England, with Stewart, the friend of his undergraduate years, and now Professor of Mathematics in Marischal College. The record of their movements in the South is scanty. Reid's uncle, Dr. George Reid, then a physician in London, provided a home for them in the metropolis; and as David Gregory, Reid's cousin, was Professor of History at Oxford, they found another home on the Isis, with an easy introduction to the colleges and social life of the great English University. The Gregory connection also opened the way to interesting things and persons at Cambridge as well as at Oxford and London. Reid, it seems, saw Bentley at Cambridge, 'who delighted him with his learning and amused him with his vanity': here, too, he enjoyed the conversation of the blind mathematician Saunderson, whose experience he afterwards turned to good account in his inquiries regarding the sense of seeing. One would like to have had Reid's first impressions of England, its metropolis, its social and church life, and its ancient colleges. It does not appear that the scenes through which he moved awakened in him much historic sentiment; that, like his contemporary Berkeley, Oxford would be the ideal home of his old age; or that he was greatly moved by its academic splendour, associated with what is noblest in English history, and by the soft repose of the surrounding rural scenes. In one of his letters to Dr. James Gregory, he speaks of the first time he was in 'Dean Gregory's house at Oxford,' when the Dean told 'the story of the watch very well to a large company of Oxonians'; so we may infer that other visits followed in later life. And the Oxford of his first visit was the degenerate Oxford described by Adam Smith and Gibbon, who were in residence a few years after. Reid is seldom again found out of Scotland. There is no sign that he ever visited Ireland or the Continent in his retired, sedate, and methodical life. In this, too, he was like Kant, who in all his eighty years is said never to have travelled more than forty miles from his native Königsberg. The stay-at-home disposition common to both is not unlike the character reflected in their books.

CHAPTER III

NEW MACHAR AND DAVID HUME

1737—1751

SOON after Reid's return to Marischal College from his English tour, the young librarian was presented, by the professors of King's College, to the pastoral charge of New Machar, a parish some ten miles to the north-west of Aberdeen. The fact that his kinsman, James Gregory, was professor in King's may perhaps explain this unwonted exercise of patronage in favour of a graduate of the rival College.

The presentation, at any rate, raised a storm of opposition among the parishioners. It was the occasion of one of those conflicts of Church parties to which the law of patronage gave rise in Scotland in those days. The incidents of Reid's introduction to ecclesiastical office form a characteristic picture. Rural prejudice was due in this case to various circumstances. It was partly influenced by a sermon, preached in the church of New Machar, on February 10, 1737, at the moderation of the call, by the Rev. John Bisset, one of the ministers of Aberdeen. Mr. Bisset had himself been minister of the parish ten years before. He was now a noted preacher in the North, and one with whom express concurrence of the congregation in an ecclesiastical settlement was a high article of doctrine.[1] In his sermon he denounced aristocratic interference, insinuated undue outside influence and personal favour, claimed a right to a vote in the election of his minister for every Christian, the poor man as much as the rich, and concluded with an appeal to his audience to quit themselves like men, and to trust in God. The recent history of the parish strengthened this appeal. The last presentation to New Machar was inauspicious. In 1729 a 'riding committee' had introduced Mr. Bisset's successor. Soon after, the new minister was accused of 'powdering his wig on the Sabbath.' Absolved by the Church courts, he was in 1736 deposed for a graver offence. It was a time of ecclesiastical anarchy in New Machar. The record of the parish is blank between the minute which tells of the departure of Mr. Bisset in 1728, and that which registers 'the ordination of Mr. Thomas Reid' in May 1737.

Reid was the innocent victim of the sermon and the scandal when he came to be ordained on May 12, 1737. He had been violently attacked and maltreated by persons in disguise, who, according to tradition, ducked him in a horse-pond. It is also told that when he officiated for the first time in the parish church, he was guarded in the pulpit by a drawn sword.

For fifteen years New Machar manse was Reid's home. Popular prejudice was overcome by his mild, beneficent activity. Those who had been carried into outrage by hasty judgment at the beginning, followed him on his departure with blessings and tears. 'We fought against Mr. Reid when he came,' they are reported

[1] In *Scotland and Scotsmen of the Eighteenth Century*, by Ramsay of Ochtertyre, there is an interesting account of this Mr. Bisset.

as saying, 'and we would have fought for him when he went away.' His marriage, in August 1740, to his cousin Elizabeth, a daughter of his London uncle, Dr. George Reid, promoted this change. The gracious manner and constant goodness of this companion of his life for more than fifty years was long remembered in the Aberdeenshire parish. Six daughters and three sons were the issue of the marriage. Five daughters were born at New Machar, and one died there. Reid's family bible at Birkwood contains the following interesting record in his handwriting :—

'Mr. Thomas Reid was born at Strachan, April 26, 1710; married to Elizabeth Reid, August 12, 1740. The said Elizabeth was born August 3, 1724. Their children :—(1) Jean, born July 21, 1741, died February 27, 1772, buried in College Churchyard, Glasgow; (2) Margaret, born October 20, 1742, died 1772, buried as above; (3) Martha, born August 22, 1744, married Dr. Patrick Carmichael; (4) Elizabeth, born February 21, 1746, died of smallpox in August 1746, buried in the Churchyard of New Machar; (5) Anna, born July 10, 1751, died of chin-cough May 21, 1753, buried in the Isle of Old Machar; (6) George, born February 11, 1755, died at St. John's, Newfoundland, February 1780; (7) Lewis, born December 13, 1756, died of teething July 19, 1758, buried in the Isle of Old Machar; (8) David, born February 26, 1762, died at Edinburgh August 30, 1782; (9) Elizabeth, born May 8, 1766, died June 1, 1767, of smallpox by inoculation, buried in the College Churchyard, Glasgow.'

The story of the fifteen years at New Machar, as we have it, is almost empty of incidents, a dim picture. The scene does not warmly touch the imagination. Undulating hills of moderate size, chill and tame; land monotonously fertile, with scanty timber; yet pleasant prospects in the distance of the valley of the Don, with Benachie and remoter Grampians in the background; a population mostly agricultural; two or three country mansions; the highroad from Aberdeen to Banff traversing the parish. New Machar was wanting, on the whole, in the breezy highland charm of the early home at Strachan. The social life was simple but intellectually stagnant. Among the infrequent visitors at the manse I find incidental mention in Reid's letters of one. He tells that he made the acquaintance of the well-known Jacobite, Mr. Hepburn of Keith, 'by his lodging a night in my house at New Machar,' when he was in the Prince's army, on his way to Culloden; perhaps when he was in Lord George Murray's division, which retreated through Aberdeenshire in February 1746, or in one of the detachments which were in motion around New Machar in the preceding December.

The Thomas Reid who is revealed to us in his books does not promise pulpit eloquence likely to interest this rustic population. Like Bishop Butler when he was in his remote rectory at Stanhope a few years before, he was pondering the chief intellectual work of his life in exile from intellectual society. None of Reid's sermons are found among his manuscripts. Indeed, it appears that his characteristic modesty and diffidence, combined, it is said, with some neglect of literary culture in his early education, induced him at first to read to his rustic audience the sermons of eminent Anglican preachers, instead of compositions of his own—thus adopting a practice afterwards recommended by Paley, by which, with fit selection, many audiences might benefit in this age of social pressure. 'As to preaching,' says Paley, 'if your situation requires a sermon every Sunday, make one and find five.' Tillotson and the Nonconformist Evans are mentioned as Reid's favourites, and something is said about Samuel Clarke. The luminous good sense of Tillotson, and the reverential temper of Evans, and the lucid reasoning of Clarke, would naturally attract Reid. But emotion as well as moral ideal was not wanting in his religious life. It is said that in a Communion Service tears fell from his eyes when he enlarged on the divine beauty of the character of Jesus. The following expression of religious feeling during an illness of his young wife appears among his manuscripts, dated March 30, 1746:—

'O God, I desire humbly to supplicate Thy Divine Majesty in behalf of my distressed wife, who is by Thy hand brought very low, and in imminent danger of death, if Thou, who alone doest wonders, do not in mercy interpose Thy almighty arm, and bring her back from the gate of death. I deserve justly, O Lord, that Thou shouldst deprive me of the greatest comfort of my life, because I have not been so thankful to Thee as I ought for giving me such a kind and affectionate wife. I have forgot Thy goodness in bringing us happily together by an unforeseen and undesigned train of events, and blessing us with so much love and harmony of affection, and so many of the comforts and conveniences of life. I have not been so careful as I ought to have been to stir her up to piety and Christian virtues. I have not taken that pains with my children and servants and relatives as I ought. Alas! I have been too negligent of my pastoral duty and my private devotions, too much given to the pleasures and satisfactions of this world, and too little influenced by the promises and the hope of a future state. I have employed my studies, reading, and conversation rather to please myself than to edify myself and others. I have sinned greatly in neglecting many opportunities of making private applications to my flock and family in the affairs of their souls, and in using too slight preparation for my public exercises. I have thrown away too much of my time in sloth and sleep, and have not done so much for the relief of the poor and destitute as I might have done. The means that Providence has afforded me of correcting my evil inclinations I have abused to pamper and feed them in various instances. For these and many other sins which have escaped my memory Thou mightst justly inflict so great a chastisement on me, as to make my children motherless and deprive me of my dear wife. O Lord, accept of my humble and penitent confession of these my offences, which I desire to acknowledge with shame and sorrow, and am resolved by Thy grace to amend. If Thou art pleased to hearken to the voice of my supplications, and grant my request on behalf of my dear wife in restoring her to health, I do promise and covenant through grace to turn from these backslidings, to express my thankfulness by a vigorous discharge of my duty as a Christian, a minister, and master of a family, and by an alms of ten pounds sterling to the poor in meat and money. Lord, pardon if there is anything in this presumptuous, or unbecoming a humble penitent sinner; and, Lord, accept of what is sincerely designed as a new bond upon my soul to my duty, through Jesus Christ, my Lord and Saviour.'

This fervid expression of devotion reveals an intensity of purpose which worked beneath the outwardly placid and discreet life. Mrs. Reid survived this critical illness for nearly half a century.

Much of Reid's time at New Machar, according to his brother-in-law Mr. Rose, was spent in meditative thought, with an attention to the activities of his own mind of which few men are capable. Traditions of solitary walks immersed in study were long in circulation. He found his chief recreation, we are told, in the manse garden or in botanical observations. His society attracted his neighbours. With Sir Archibald Grant of Monymusk he maintained a lifelong intimacy. He never forgot New Machar, and long after, in times of distress, anonymous gifts were traced to his thoughtful but modest beneficence.

Three years before Reid left New Machar, when he was in his thirty-eighth year, he made his first appearance in print, in a short paper contributed to the Royal Society, which appeared in their *Transactions* in October 1748. It is called 'An Essay on Quantity.' It was occasioned by a book published more than twenty years before, the *Inquiry into the Original of our Ideas of Beauty and Virtue*, by Francis Hutcheson, afterwards the celebrated Professor of Moral Philosophy in Glasgow. In this tract simple and compound ratios are applied, in forms of mathematical reasoning, to solve problems of moral philosophy. It illustrates in some degree the bent of Reid's thoughts at this time, and his inherited interest in mathematical reasonings. But it also shows bent of thought in another direction, and recognition of other scientific methods than mathematical demonstration, which had been favoured as of universal application by philosophers like Descartes and Spinoza. Reid argued, in the spirit of his master Turnbull, that genuine ethical inquiry is concerned with a class of facts which are under a higher category, and refuse to submit to geometrical measurement.

It is a curious circumstance in the evolution of philosophy in Scotland that Reid's first publication should thus be adverse criticism of Hutcheson, the father of Modern Philosophy in Scotland. It is also curious that this juvenile performance presents another of the parallels between Reid and Kant. For it happened that in the preceding year Kant had made his first appearance, on a question concerned with mathematics, and, like Reid's, in an argument against conclusions maintained by Leibnitz.

But this mathematical *brochure* imperfectly represents the 'intense study' at New Machar. For an event happened soon after Reid's settlement there which determined the direction of his thoughts for the remainder of his life. In January 1739, a book made an almost unnoticed appearance in London, which in the end became the chief factor in shaping the course of European thought. Its author was David Hume, then a young man, unknown to fame, not thirty years of age, the younger son of a Berwickshire laird. Hume was younger than Reid by one year: both were born on the 26th of April. His name is popularly connected with the *History of England*; but this *Treatise of Human Nature*, which somehow found its way into the manse of New Machar, represents his most significant work. It has contributed perhaps as much as any single book to the subsequent progress of philosophy in Europe. Hume indeed penetrates into regions which the ordinary reader fails to connect with everyday interests of life, or with the hopes and fears of human beings. Accordingly, as he tells, the *Treatise* 'fell dead-born from the press, without attaining such distinction as even to excite a murmur among the zealots.' In a letter to his friend Henry Home, afterwards Lord Kames, written soon after this explosive mixture had been applied, its author announces that the issue was 'but indifferent, if I may judge by the sale of the book, and if I may believe my bookseller. I am now out of humour with myself; but doubt not in a little time to be out of humour with the world, like other unsuccessful authors. After all, I am sensible of my folly in entertaining any discontent, much more despair, on this account, since I could not expect any better from such abstract reasoning.' This book, which professes to explain 'human nature' as a fact in the universe, conducts to a final paralysis of human intelligence in universal doubt.

This threatened paralysis awoke Reid into his characteristic intellectual life. He was among the first in Europe to see the far-reaching meaning of Hume's account of man's condition. He found in it the deep-lying seeds of modern agnosticism. Its rashness was confessed by its author. 'I acknowledge a very great mistake in conduct in publishing my *Treatise of Human Nature*, a book which pretended to innovate in all the sublimest parts of philosophy, and which I composed before I was five-and-twenty. But what success the same doctrines better illustrated and expressed may meet with *adhuc sub judice lis est*. I wish I had always confined myself to the more easy parts of erudition.' Accordingly, about ten years after, Hume presented his 'sceptical doubts' in a milder form, and accompanied by a 'sceptical solution' of them, in an *Inquiry Concerning Human Understanding*; but it was Hume in the original *Treatise*, not as recast in the *Inquiry*, that moved Reid. Kant, like Reid, was awakened from what he calls his 'dogmatic slumber' by David Hume; but it was the *Inquiry*, not the *Treatise*, of which last he appears ignorant, that roused Kant. Reid grappled with the more open and all-pervading uncertainties of the earlier work.

Let us look into the book which appalled the young minister of New Machar by the spectre of a meaningless universe and illusory human nature. Its author seemed to be indulging in 'a peculiar strain of humour when he set out in his introduction by promising with a grave face no less than a complete system of the sciences upon a foundation entirely new, namely, human nature, while the intention of the whole work is to show that there is neither human nature nor science in the world. He surely believed, against his principles, that he should be read, and that he should retain his personal identity till he reaped the reputation justly due to his metaphysical acumen.' Reid found him taking for granted as his fundamental maxim, that nothing can be admitted as true which cannot be logically deduced from impressions of sense. Hume found the impressions of sense to be transitory, and distinguished in their succession by degrees of intensity,—sensations when in their highest intensity, memories when in an abated degree, and mere fancies when the intensity is at a minimum. His maxim forbade recognition of more reality in the universe than a momentary reality of isolated perceptions, in their different degrees of intensity, but without any reasonable retrospective memory, or any reasonable expectation with its hopes or fears. What we call 'existence' was resolved into an unintelligible chaos of felt impressions—a purposeless procession, in which the percipient loses his very selfhood and all besides. The Past, the Distant, the Future, are all illusions. 'Things' and 'persons' are only unconnected transitory feelings, without any permanent person to feel them. The word 'identity' is meaningless. A person cannot be more than a momentary idea. 'I never catch *self* except in the form of a passing feeling.' Present feeling alone exists.

It is impossible without contradiction to express a philosophy which destroys intelligible expression; virtually dismissing as absurdities all personal pronouns, all substantive nouns, and all verbs; leaving abstract adjectives as the only parts of speech;—and, as such adjectives are really unintelligible, leaving us the speechless and motionless victims of philosophical suicide. When I start with the preliminary maxim of Hume, I literally lose 'myself' at last in a radically untrustworthy universe, or I find myself suspended over a bottomless abyss. Here are the last words of this intellectual suicide at the end of his destructive analysis :—

'I am affrighted and confounded with the forlorn solitude in which I am placed by my philosophy. When we trace up the human understanding to its first principles, we find it to lead us into such sentiments as seem to turn into ridicule all our past pains and industry, and to discourage us from all future inquiries. Nothing is more curiously inquired after by the mind of man than the *causes* of phenomena ; nor are we content with knowing the immediate causes, but push on our inquiries till we arrive at the original and ultimate principle. This is our aim in all our studies and reflections. And now we must be disappointed when we learn that this tie lies merely in ourselves, and is nothing but that determination which is acquired by custom. Such a discovery not only cuts off all hope of ever attaining satisfaction, but even prevents our very wishes ; since it appears that when we desire to know the ultimate and operating principle or something which resides in the external object, we only contradict ourselves, or talk without a meaning. . . . The intense view of these manifold contradictions and imperfections in human reason has so wrought upon me and heated my brain, that I am ready to reject all belief and reasoning, and can look at no opinion even as more probable or likely than another. All who believe anything, on any subject, with certainty, must be fools.'

This is the issue of the *Treatise of Human Nature* when the logical understanding is finally resolved into transitory and isolated feelings, without permitted final postulates of reason, in the form of faith or in any other form, to connect and interpret them.

It was this issue that Reid took seriously. He set himself, at first for his own satisfaction only, to consider the ground he had for trusting experience, when Hume reported that experience dissolved into sensational atoms. Accordingly he spent much of his time at New Machar in reflecting first of all on his perceptions through the senses. He began with these, because it seemed that even as the foundations of abstract mathematics lie in the mathematical axioms and definitions, so the foundations of all concrete reasoning are to be found in the rational constitution of perception through the five senses. 'In the tree of human knowledge, perception is the root, common understanding is the trunk, and the sciences are the branches.' Here is his own account of his state of mind when he was engaged in these New Machar wrestlings :—

'If my mind is indeed what the *Treatise of Human Nature* makes it, I find that I have been only in an enchanted castle, when I seemed to be living in a well-ordered universe. I have been imposed upon by spectres and apparitions. I blush inwardly to think how I have been deluded. I am ashamed of my frame, and can hardly forbear expostulating with my destiny. I see myself, and the whole frame of Nature, shrink into fleeting ideas, which, like Epicurus's atoms, dance about in emptiness. Descartes no sooner began to dig in this mine than scepticism was ready to break in upon him. He did what he could to keep it out. Malebranche and Locke, who dug deeper, found the difficulty of keeping out the enemy still to increase; but they laboured honestly in the design. Then Berkeley, who carried on the work, despairing of securing all, bethought himself of an expedient. By giving up the material world, which he thought might be spared without loss, and even with advantage, he hoped by an impregnable position to secure the world of spirits. But, alas! the *Treatise of Human Nature* wantonly sapped the foundation of this partition, and drowned all in one universal deluge.'

Nearly forty years after he left New Machar, Reid says[1] that in early life he 'believed the whole of Berkeley's system'—till Hume opened his eyes to 'consequences' that follow from the philosophy of Descartes and his successors, 'which gave me more uneasiness than the want of a material world. So it came into my mind more than forty years ago' to question its foundation. Hume accordingly made Reid revise critically the philosophy in which he had been educated by George Turnbull. The issue appeared after he left New Machar.

[1] *Essays on the Intellectual Powers*, II. ch. 10.

Reid was now to be placed in a condition more favourable to intense and persistent thought. On November 22, 1751, he was admitted to King's College, Aberdeen, as one of its regent masters, in succession to Mr. Alexander Rait. The patronage was vested in the College, and the minute which records his election suggests the reputation which the rural pastor had now secured among the cultured few, notwithstanding his modest and retired life.

It was not without reluctance that Reid left New Machar. Ramsay of Ochtertyre, who knew him well, tells that when the deputation from King's College came to invite him to become a regent, 'he at first declined, explaining that he desired to live in retirement till he should complete some literary projects which engaged him. Mrs. Reid, however, having discovered the errand of the visitors, urged her husband to accept the offer, being less fond of retirement, and having no objection to a better income and better society. When her learned guests repeated their proposal after dinner, she seconded them with such cogent arguments that Mr. Reid was beat out of all his objections.'—*Scotland and Scotsmen.*

CHAPTER IV

OLD ABERDEEN: A REGENT IN KING'S COLLEGE

1751—1764

REID'S movement from New Machar to the academic home opened for him in Old Aberdeen placed him and his young family amidst surroundings that touch imagination by their natural beauty and historic associations. For centuries the College, founded by Bishop Elphinstone, and at first presided over by Hector Boece, with its chapel and crowned tower, in the

> old university town,
> Between the Don and the Dee,
> Looking over the grey sand dunes,
> Looking out on the cold North Sea,

has shed intellectual light over the North of Scotland, especially among the Celts in the Highlands. At King's College one sees a miniature Oxford almost under the shadow of the Grampians. Perhaps Reid's temperament was too prosaic to contemplate his new surroundings with the sentiment which the city at the mouth of the Don afterwards called forth in Thackeray, who, in 'a delightful tour in the north, was charmed with Inverness, and fell in love with Old Aberdeen—an elderly decayed mouldering old beauty who lives quietly on the seashore, near her grand new granite sister of a city.' The affectionate recollection with which Sir James Mackintosh recalled his student days at King's College, and the companionship there of Robert Hall, is another testimony to its charms. The arena in which these two, called by their fellow-students 'Plato and Herodotus,' encountered one another most frequently was in morals and metaphysics. 'After having sharpened their weapons by reading, they often repaired to the spacious sands upon the seashore, and still more to the picturesque scenery on the banks of the Don above the old town and the Brig of Balgownie, to discuss with eagerness the problems of existence. There was scarcely an important position in Berkeley's *Minute Philosopher*, in Butler's *Analogy*, or in *Edwards on the Will*, over which they did not debate with the utmost intensity.' From these discussions in the environs of the 'old university town,' Mackintosh was wont to say that he 'learned more than from all the books he ever read.'

It was in the canonist's manse, pleasantly placed nearly in front of the College, immediately north of the Snow Church, at the entrance to Powis House, that Reid found himself in the winter of 1751.[1] It was rented by him from the University. The quaint manse, nestled among trees, with its low thatched roof,[2] has disappeared, and with it other picturesque old houses, which added charm to the neighbourhood when Reid taught in King's College nearly a hundred and fifty years ago. The crown tower of the College chapel rose almost in front of the manse, the rival of St. Giles's at Edinburgh and of St. Nicholas's at Newcastle, unique in Scottish academical architecture. Eastwards in the quadrangle was the Hall in which the students

[1] While he lived here, he seems to have retained the incumbency of New Machar till May 1752.
[2] Long ago removed. I have an engraving of it.

dined, a memorial of Bishop Elphinstone, and the dormitories of the students, which were of later date. General Monk's tower stood in the eastern corner; behind the Hall was the kitchen, and near it the College well, whence the links stretched to the shore, 'the grey sand dunes' in those days unbroken by tame streets and modern villas.

The professorial system of divided work, which assigns special departments of learning to supposed experts, had not superseded in King's College the method of regency which prevailed in the early history of all the universities of Scotland. The regent was intrusted with the education of his pupils from the first matriculation to graduation; or when Latin, Greek, and pure mathematics were each provided for professorially, regents in philosophy each taught in successive sessions the various branches of natural and physical science, and of moral and metaphysical philosophy. This system was followed in all the Scottish universities until last century. It was modified by the Commission of 1690, which ordained that, besides a separate professor of Latin, one of the four regents should profess Greek only, and take charge of undergraduates in their first year. By about the middle of the century 'regenting' was wholly abolished in four of the five Universities—in Edinburgh in 1708, in Glasgow in 1727, in St. Andrews in 1747, and in Marischal College and University in 1753. But in King's College the various branches of Philosophy, natural and moral, were still regented when Reid began to teach. He was thus required to teach mathematics and the sciences of matter, as well as psychology and moral philosophy. He thus gave lectures on the philosophy of mind only every third year. One of the other two years was given to natural history and the easier parts of physical science; the second to mathematics and natural philosophy.

During 1751-52, which was his first session, Reid as regent taught natural philosophy to undergraduates of the third year; in the following winter the same students, in their fourth year, were still in his charge. His full sequence, accordingly, did not commence till 1753-54, when for the first time he took the second class, consisting of those beginning philosophical studies. So his successive three years courses ran thus:—1753-56, 1756-59, 1759-62. In the last year of each course, as 'promoter,' he presented his undergraduates to receive the Master's degree, and also delivered a graduation thesis. His theses (still extant in manuscript at Birkwood) were in Latin; they deal chiefly with the methods and human conditions of philosophical inquiry.

Two-thirds of Reid's lectures at King's College were in this way concerned with natural history and applied mathematics: only one-third was given to the central object of his intellectual interest at New Machar. I have examined a manuscript volume of notes of the lectures in 'Natural Philosophy' which he gave in 1757-58. They comprehend, after an introductory exposition of the province and methods of physics, the laws of motion, astronomy, optics, electricity, and hydrostatics. The notes show that Reid was well abreast of the physical science of his time.

At the time of Reid's appointment as a regent of philosophy in King's College, the alternative of regency or professoriate was discussed in the University. He entered readily into this and other questions of University reform, and prevailed on his colleagues to make some important changes. Largely through his influence the teaching session was extended from five to seven months; the Humanity or Latin class was better organised; the bursary endowments were redistributed for competition; and in the order of undergraduate study, the sciences concerned with the outward world were made to precede psychology and ethics, which were reserved for the last year, as more consistent with the development of the human mind in its natural ascent from external observation to reflection. An account of the changes was published in 1754.

It is curious that it was through Reid's influence that the regency system was retained in King's College, in preference to the professorial, which, in order to secure division of labour among the teachers, under the growth of knowledge, had been already adopted in the other Universities. His hand may be traced in the following statement of reasons for this conservative policy :—' Every professor of philosophy in this University is also tutor to those who study under him; and it seems to be generally agreed that it must be detrimental to a student to change his every session. And though it be allowed that a professor who has only one branch of philosophy for his province may have more leisure to make improvements in it for the benefit of the learned world, yet it does not seem extravagant to suppose that a [regent] professor ought to be sufficiently qualified to teach all that his pupils can learn in philosophy [natural and moral] in the course of three sessions.' Half a century later the higher academical ideal implied in a professoriate prevailed, according to which the professor is responsible for promoting his branch of human knowledge, as well as for the instruction of youth—in educating influence more powerful, when he incites to study by the vitality which original research is apt to communicate to his lectures. The development of a university, it has been remarked, is prompt and easy when each department of its cyclopædia is separately taught by an able professor; whereas a university which abandons instruction to regent-tutors must be content not only to teach little, and that little ill, but to continue to teach what is elsewhere obsolete and exploded.

In a letter of Reid's in 1755, an account is given of the reformed, if somewhat officious, academical discipline which then prevailed:—

'The students here,' he says, 'have lately been compelled to live within the College. We need but look out at our windows to see when they rise and when they go to bed. They are seen nine or ten times throughout the day statedly, by one or other of the Masters—at public prayers, school-hours, meals, in their rooms, besides occasional visits which we can make with little trouble to ourselves. They are shut up within walls at nine at night. This discipline hath indeed taken some pains and resolution, as well as some expense, to establish it. The board of the first table is 50 marks per quarter, *i.e.* 54s. 2d., and the second 40. The rent of a room is from 7 shillings to 20 shillings in the session. There is no furniture in their rooms but a bedstead, tables, chimney-grate, and fender; the rest they must buy for themselves. All other perquisites from 12 to 17 shillings.'

This discipline was more or less in vogue during the remainder of last century. Nearly twenty years after the date of Reid's letter, when Johnson and Boswell visited Aberdeen, Johnson says that 'in King's College there is kept a public table, but the scholars in the Marischal College are boarded in the town.' 'The abandonment of this custom,' Mr. Rait tells us, 'seems to have been a gradual process, and to have taken place during the first quarter of the nineteenth century. The restraint of collegiate residence had become exceedingly irksome.' With the increasing age of entrants, schoolboy discipline might seem less expedient.

Instruction in the art of dancing was, it seems, provided by the University under the reformed regulations, to add manly grace to the rude bodily vigour of the Scottish undergraduate. Reid in advocating this may have remembered Locke's advice in his *Thoughts on Education*: 'Dancing being that which gives graceful motions all the life, and above all things manliness and a becoming confidence, I think it cannot be learned too early. But you must be sure to have a good master, that knows and can teach what is graceful and becoming, and that gives a freedom and ease to all the motions of the body. One that teaches not this is worse than none at all.' How long this civilising art was cultivated in Reid's College I have not discovered.

In Aberdeen Reid found himself in the society of persons of more than provincial eminence, destined, indeed, to leave their mark on the thought and literature of Scotland. The Chair of Medicine in his College was occupied by his cousin, Dr. John Gregory, a successful observer of external nature and man. In Marischal College, Thomas Blackwell, the Professor of Greek when Reid was an undergraduate, was now Principal; soon followed by George Campbell, who became the philosophical theologian of the Church of Scotland, by his criticism of Hume's reasoning about miracles, and a master in literary, biblical, and ecclesiastical criticism,—in his *Philosophy of Rhetoric*, his Translation of the Gospels, and his History of the development of the Christian Church. Campbell was nine years younger than Reid, like him an alumnus of Marischal College; he had been minister of Banchory-Ternan for nine years before he was called to Aberdeen. He rivalled Reid himself in analytic power and calm, candid, luminous reasoning. Alexander Gerard, like Reid, a University reformer, and author of essays on 'Taste' and on 'Genius,' was Professor of Philosophy in Marischal College, and then of Divinity there, and afterwards at King's. There was William Duncan, too, whose *Logic* was for a time in vogue in Scottish Universities —a regent in Marischal College when Reid began to teach philosophy at King's; and Reid's lifelong friend Stewart was still in the Chair of Mathematics. Perhaps the most widely known Aberdonian when he lived was James Beattie, poet more than philosopher, Professor of Logic and Moral Philosophy in Marischal College, whose essay on 'Truth' gave him a name in the intellectual world, while the grace and pathos of the 'Minstrel' and the 'Hermit' appealed to a wider class, and secured a popular reputation. Aberdeen and its neighbourhood were then the home also of accomplished physicians and naturalists and scholars— Skenes and Ogilvies, Dunbars and Gordons.

As I have said, Reid's first years at King's College were much given to academical reform. His later years there were distinguished by his connection with a Society for philosophical inquiry, then quickened in Scotland by the fashionable scepticism of David Hume. Reid and Gregory originated this 'Aberdeen Philosophical Society,' or 'Wise Club,' as it was called. It was the parent of some of the most remarkable books in Scottish philosophical literature in the latter part of last century. The first meeting was on January 12, 1758, and the last was in February 1773. The original members were Dr. John Gregory, Dr. David Skene, Professor John Stewart, Mr. Robert Trail, the Rev. George

Campbell, and Mr. Thomas Reid; to whom in the same year were added the Rev. Alexander Gerard, the Rev. John Farquhar, Mr. Charles Gordon, and Mr. John Kerr. James Beattie joined them in 1760, Dr. George Skene and Mr. William Ogilvie in 1763, Mr. James Dunbar in 1765, and Mr. William Trail in 1766. Reid was secretary of the Society, and the minutes for many years are in his handwriting. It met once a fortnight on the second and fourth Wednesdays of each month. 'The members,' Sir W. Forbes tells us in his *Life of Beattie*, 'met at five o'clock in the evening—for in those days at Aberdeen it was the custom to dine early—when one of the members, as president, took the chair, and left it at half an hour after eight, when they partook of a slight and inexpensive collation, and at ten o'clock they separated.' At these meetings it appears that part of the evening's entertainment was the reading of a short essay, composed by one of the members in his turn. Besides these discourses, a literary or philosophical question was proposed each night, for discussion at the next meeting. And it was the duty of the proposer of the question to open the discussion; by him, also, the opinions of the members who took a part in it were digested into an abstract, which was engrossed in the album of the Society. I am told that the *Lion Inn*, on the Spital Hill near Reid's manse, and sometimes the *Lemon Tree Inn*, in the new town, were the usual places of meeting. The common attendance was five or six. One of the rules enjoined moderation and forbade toasts.

The meetings were given partly to essays by the members, and partly to oral discussions of proposed questions. 'Philosophy,' according to the rules, 'comprehends every principle of science which may be deduced by just or lawful induction from the phenomena either of the human mind or of the material world.' Perhaps no society of the kind in this country has fulfilled its end so well. The 'Rankenian Club' and the 'Select Society' in Edinburgh lasted longer, or enrolled more members, but neither of them was the parent of so much good literature. The 'Inquiry' of Reid, Beattie's essay on 'Truth,' Gerard on 'Taste' and on 'Genius,' and Campbell's books on 'Miracles' and on 'Rhetoric' appear in fragments or in germ in the minutes of the 'Wise Club' of Aberdeen. Its vitality was sustained and stimulated by the sceptical speculations of Hume, which were much in touch with educated opinion in the third quarter of last century, when spiritual philosophy was languid in Britain and throughout the world. The tone of those engaged in the philosophical vindication of belief appears in one of Reid's letters, who writes thus to David Hume in 1763:—

'Your friendly adversaries, Drs. Campbell and Gerard, as well as Dr. Gregory, return their compliments to you respectfully. A little Philosophical Society here, of which all three are members, is much indebted to you for its entertainment. Your company, although we are all good Christians, would be more acceptable than that of Athanasius; and since we cannot have you upon the bench, you are brought oftener than any other man to the bar; accused and defended with great zeal, but without bitterness. If you write no more in morals, politics, and metaphysics, I am afraid we shall be at a loss for subjects.'

It is interesting to find in the records of the Society the subjects of the dissertations contributed by Reid during the six years in which he was its mainspring,[1] as well as the questions which he proposed for debate. They signally

[1] These MS. dissertations have been lately recovered, and I have thus been able to compare them with the *Inquiry*, in which I find them mostly embodied.

illustrate the course of his thoughts in these years. On May 24, 1758, 'Mr. Reid intimat that he designed as the subject of his discourse some Observations on the Philosophy of the Mind, and particularly on the Perceptions we have by Sight.' On June 17, 1758, he read a paper 'On the Difficulty of a just Philosophy of the Human Mind; General Prejudices against D——d (*sic*) Hume's System of the Mind; and some Observations on the Perceptions we have by Sight.' On March 14, 1759, he presented an 'Analysis of the Sensations of Smell and Taste.' On 26th February 1760 'Mr. Reid intimat that in his discourse he was to continue his Analysis of the Senses'; and accordingly, on the 20th of August in the same year, he gave notice of his intention of 'taking Dr. Gregory's place and reading a paper on the Sense of Touch.' In July 1761 he appears with a paper on the 'Transit of Venus' in that year; and on the 26th January 1762 he gives a 'Valedictory Address,' as first annual president of the Society (the members having previously taken the chair by rotation)—on 'Euclid's Definitions and Axioms,' in which he returns to the favourite studies of his youth. In 1761 he had resumed his investigation of the Senses, for in September he is credited with another paper on the 'Sense of Seeing.' His last contribution, in October 1762, was on 'Perception,' which summed up his characteristic work in the Society. And after reading this paper, 'Mr. Reid declined to give it for insertion in the Records, in regard that he proposed soon to send it to the press, along with some other discourses which he had read before the Society.' A minute on 28th October 1764 announces that, 'as Dr. Reid has left this country, no discourse is to be expected from him.'

The following Questions for debate were proposed by Reid

during the six years of his membership:—1758, 13th and 26th July, 'Are the Objects of the Human Mind properly divided into Impressions and Ideas; and must every Idea be a copy of a preceding Impression?' This closely touches the fundamental assumption of the sceptical philosophy. Those which follow suggest a disposition to ethical and social discussion. 12th June 1759, 'Whether Mankind with regard to Morals always was and is the same?' 1st April 1760, 'Whether it is proper to educate Children without instilling Principles into them of any kind whatever?' (Beattie's celebrated experiment in the education of his son may be connected with this.) 15th April 1761, 'Whether Moral Character consists in Affections in which the Will is not concerned, or in fixed, habitual, and constant Purposes?' 8th January 1762, 'Whether by the encouragement of proper Laws the Number of Births in Great Britain might be nearly doubled, or at least greatly increased?' Here we have a sort of inverted Malthusianism suggested. 22nd November 1763, 'Whether every Action deserving Moral Approbation must be done from a persuasion of its being morally good?'

Beattie, in one of his letters to Sir W. Forbes, thus refers to the Society and to his own philosophical relation to Reid:—

'I have of late been much engaged in metaphysics; at least, I have been labouring with all my might to overturn that visionary science. I am a member of a club in this town who style themselves the Philosophical Society. I hope you will not think the worse of this Society when I tell you, that to it the world is indebted for a *Comparative View of the Faculties of Man*, and an *Inquiry into Human Nature on the Principles of Common Sense*. I have shown that all genuine reasoning does ultimately terminate in principles which it is impossible to disbelieve, and as impossible to prove; that, therefore, the ultimate standard of truth to us is Common Sense, or that instinctive conviction into which all true reasoning does resolve itself; that therefore what contradicts Common Sense is in itself absurd, however subtle the arguments which support it. My principles in the main are not essentially different from Dr. Reid's; but they seem to offer a more compendious method of destroying scepticism. I intend to show (and have already in part shown) that all sophistical reasoning is marked by certain characters which distinguish it from true investigation; and thus I flatter myself I shall be able to discover a method of detecting sophistry, even when one is not able to give a logical confutation of its arguments.'

Beattie argued more in the temper of a partisan than Reid, who criticised Hume in the spirit of a free and candid inquirer after truth.

On the 18th of January 1762 the honorary Doctorate of Divinity was conferred on Reid by Marischal College.

His fame was now more than local. In December 1763 he accepted the invitation of the University of Glasgow to fill the Chair of Moral Philosophy which Adam Smith had resigned. Before he entered on this new career he had given to the world an *Inquiry into the Human Mind on the Principles of Common Sense*. This classic work embodies the result of twenty years of steady reflection at New Machar and Aberdeen, in quest of the actual foundation of human knowledge. Before we follow him to Glasgow, we must examine this issue of his intellectual life in Aberdeenshire—due to the challenge of modern agnosticism in the person of David Hume.

CHAPTER V

UNIVERSAL SCEPTICISM VERSUS INSPIRED COMMON SENSE: AN 'INQUIRY INTO THE HUMAN MIND ON THE PRINCIPLES OF COMMON SENSE'

1764

As early as October 1762, as we have seen, Reid had given signs of an intention to offer the world some results of his meditations regarding the foundations of belief. Accordingly, in the end of the following year, he produced his first book, *An Inquiry into the Human Mind on the Principles of Common Sense*. Its motto expresses its leading argument—'The inspiration of the Almighty giveth them understanding.' For it was to the inspirations, or revelations, of what he called the 'common sense' or 'common judgment,' regarded as the root of any human understanding of man and his environment, that he made his final appeal against the all-embracing doubt of Hume. This was the rock on which he took his stand in the universal deluge.

Reid was now in his fifty-fourth year. Hitherto his modesty had concealed his strength from all but a few friends. His book was concerned with questions that were not likely to withdraw him rapidly from 'the obscurity of a learned retirement.' The *Inquiry*, with its appeal to the final reason latent in human nature, is not to be interpreted as an appeal to popular opinion against theories of philosophers. In fact, its implied argument is not obvious to popular intelligence, although it is profoundly connected with all the chief interests of human life. Great books of this sort attract only the few who think. His brother-in-law, Mr. Rose, mentions that 'Alexander Millar, the London bookseller, being in Aberdeen at this time, and in company with Dr. Reid, protested against books in metaphysics as bad bargains for publishers; by which he said he had himself lost money, but never gained any. Notwithstanding, Dr. Reid, having his *Inquiry* ready for publication, sold it to Mr. Millar for £50. When his friends bantered him upon the small sum he had received for so valuable a performance, he jocosely replied, "I think it is well sold."'[1]

Another parallel here occurs between Reid and Kant. The *Kritik of Pure Reason*, Kant's first great work, appeared in 1781, when he was in his fifty-seventh year. So, too, with Locke, who inaugurated the era of modern thought in which Reid and Kant are chief figures. His *Essay*, like Reid's *Inquiry*, was the first fruit of twenty years of reflective thought, and it too made its appearance when its author was in his fifty-seventh year. It is curious to contrast the balanced caution and moderation of these long pondered treatises with the more paradoxical productions of others, whose intellectual ardour and impatience speedily committed them to all-comprehensive systems. Descartes, at forty, with his provisional doubt and reconstruction on a slender foundation; Spinoza, younger still, with his rational evolution of the universe from a single substance; Berkeley with his analysis of the material world into significant ideas, delivered at the age of twenty-five

[1] Birkwood MS.

with the impetuous enthusiasm of Irish juvenile genius; and David Hume with his universal disintegration of human knowledge and belief, planned before he was one-and-twenty, composed before he was twenty-five, and eagerly given to the world in his twenty-eighth year. Reid, with his 'good and well-wearing parts,' characteristically represents the restrained authorship of those who treat our short life on this planet as short enough for well-weighed answers to the final questions about life and the universe.

As Reid's *Inquiry* was really an appeal to human nature in arrest of Hume's intellectual suicide, he desired, before presenting it to the world, to submit the argument privately to the Edinburgh sceptic. This was done through their common friend Dr. Blair. After Hume had read portions of the manuscript, he wrote this courteous letter to Reid on Feb. 25, 1763:—

'By Dr. Blair's means I have been favoured with the perusal of your performance, which I have read with great pleasure and attention. It is certainly very rare that a piece so deeply philosophical is wrote with so much spirit, and affords so much entertainment to the reader, though I must still regret the disadvantages under which I read it, as I never had the whole performance at once before me, and could not be able to compare one part with another. To this reason chiefly I ascribe some obscurities which, in spite of your short analysis and abstract, seem to hang over your system; for I must do you the justice to own that when I enter into your ideas, no man appears to express himself with greater perspicuity than you do, a talent which above all others is requisite in that species of literature which you have cultivated. There are some objections which I would willingly propose to the chapter "Of Sight," did I not suspect that they arise from my not sufficiently understanding it. I shall therefore forbear till the whole can lie before me, and shall not at present propose any further difficulties to your reasonings. I shall only say that if you have been able to clear up these abstruse and important subjects, instead of being mortified, I shall be so vain as to pretend to a share of the praise; and shall think that my errors, by having at least some coherence, have led you to make a more strict review of my principles, which were the common ones, and to perceive their futility.'

In his reply to this letter Reid recognises the debt which philosophy owes to the sceptical criticism of Hume. He writes thus to Hume:—

'KING'S COLLEGE, 18*th March* 1763.

'SIR,—On Monday last Mr. John Farquhar brought me your letter of February 25th, enclosed in one from Dr. Blair. I thought myself very happy in having the means of obtaining, at second hand, through the friendship of Dr. Blair, your opinion of my performance; and you have been pleased to communicate it directly in so polite and friendly a manner as merits great acknowledgments on my part.

'In attempting to throw some light on these abstruse subjects, I wish to preserve the due mean between confidence and despair. But whether I have any success in this attempt or not, I shall always avow myself your disciple in metaphysics. I have learned more from your writings in this kind than from all others put together. Your system appears to me not only coherent in all its parts, but likewise justly deduced from principles commonly received among philosophers,—principles which I never thought of calling in question, until the conclusions you draw from them in the *Treatise of Human Nature* made me suspect them. If these principles are solid your system must stand; and whether they are or not can better be judged after you have brought to light the whole system that grows out of them, than when the greater part of it was wrapped up in clouds and darkness. I agree with you therefore, that if this system shall ever be demolished, you have a just claim to a great share of the praise, both because you have made it a distinct and determinate mark to be aimed at, and have furnished proper artillery for the purpose. When you have seen the whole of my performance, I shall take it as a very great favour to have your opinion upon it, from which I make no doubt of receiving light, whether I receive conviction or no.'

Hume's philosophy being the suicide of intelligence, can hardly be spoken of as a 'system.' It is not constructive, but wholly destructive, and therefore a negation of system, philosophic or other, in a finally speechless and motionless agnostic doubt.

Hume's letter to Reid was his only rejoinder to the *Inquiry*. In 1763 he had ceased to produce philosophical books. His recognition of the 'deeply philosophical' nature of Reid's argument is a testimony to the worth of the work on which Reid's literary reputation chiefly rests. The 'share of the praise' which Hume claims, Reid was ready to concede. 'I hope,' he says in the Dedication of the *Inquiry*, 'I hope that the author of this sceptical system wrote it in the belief that it would be useful to mankind. And perhaps it may prove so at last. For I conceive the sceptical writers to be a set of men whose business it is to pick holes in the fabric of knowledge wherever it is weak and faulty; and when those places are properly repaired, the whole building becomes more firm and solid than it was formerly.' And, in fact, the intellectual progress of mankind has been sustained by an alternation of sceptical and conservative philosophies.

After prolonged cogitation, the 'weak and faulty' place in the 'fabric' of modern philosophy seemed to Reid to lie in an unproved assumption with which modern philosophers set out in their speculations. For they took for granted that only the sensations and ideas within each mind could be perceived: yet we naturally 'believe that we are seeing and handling the very outward things themselves' that make what is called the material world. If the philosophers are right, we have no immediate revelation of the qualities of outward things, and no evidence of their existence, except the succession of changing sensations and ideas of sensations which alone are presented to us. I can never directly encounter an external object. What I suppose to be outward is all in my mind. With a world thus imprisoned within me, is there any legitimate way through which I can assure myself of realities outside my mind, including other living persons who have their own sensations and ideas as much as I have mine, but numerically different from my private stock? If not, grave consequences seemed to follow: faith and hope must die out of human life. So Reid argued.

The *Treatise of Human Nature* was the scarecrow that warned Reid of the destructive consequences of this assumption, that we are shut up among our own ideas; as he had himself in youth been taught to believe, and by which he had been led on to Berkeley's conception of a wholly ideal material world. He now began to see this ideal material world of Berkeley in a new light. It seemed to leave him *alone* in the universe of his own mind. The ideal matter of Berkeley cannot, he argued, inform me of the existence of other living persons: what I have supposed to be other persons must be, like the rest, only some of my own ideas. If I allow that my own sensations and ideas are my only possible original data, I cannot from such transitory phantoms infer the real existence of other persons. With this starting-point as my only one, the whole universe naturally supposed to surround me—bodies and spirits, friends and relations, all dead things and all living persons—acknowledged by common judgment to have a permanent existence, whether I am having ideas of them or not—vanish at once. My *private* sensations and ideas can never really signify to me the existence of other conscious beings; only what might be called *public ideas*, common to other minds and to me, could do this. And such objects are not properly called 'ideas'—public or private; they are dead things and living persons; they exist whether I individually have sensations and ideas or not. In short, Reid could find nothing in Berkeley's philosophical theory—as he interpreted it[1]—which afforded even probable ground for concluding that there were in existence other intelligent beings—fathers, brothers, friends, or fellow-citizens. 'I am left alone,' the only creature of God, in that forlorn state of egoism into which it was said some of the disciples of Descartes were brought by this same preliminary assumption of their master—a sufficient *reductio ad absurdum* of the favourite postulate which leads to it. To act upon it would argue insanity in the agent; it must therefore be empty verbal speculation. So Reid further argued.

But even this solitude is not the last issue of Reid's *bête noire*. The system in which I have been educated, he said, not only leaves me absolutely alone; *it extinguishes me*, along with the external universe of things and persons; it is at last literally suicidal. It transforms persistent personal existence into a mere succession of unconnected sensations and ideas. If the magic circle of sensations and ideas, within a self that persists amidst perpetual changes, cannot be broken through, then even this supposed 'self' must be an illusion, and the word self must be meaningless. The personal pronoun 'I,' as well as the personal pronoun 'you,' are both alike unmeaning. The universe resolves at last, not merely into sensations that are all referable to myself, but into sensations without any self—into isolated sensations—which seem indeed to follow one another in

[1] I have elsewhere discussed the true meaning of Berkeley's philosophy.

an orderly way, but without any guarantee that the seeming order is more than transitory, or that the illusory cosmos may not at any moment become chaos.

Is there nothing within the resources of reason to arrest this intellectual suicide? Has reason got anything to show in justification of this preliminary sacrifice of a conviction on which men have to act, whatever their theories may be? Must I surrender the conviction, that when I am seeing or touching I am actually having revealed to me something that is extended and solid, and that, *as such*, *must* be more and other than the private sensations and ideas of the person that is seeing and touching? Must this conviction, and others like it, on which human experience practically depends, be all sacrificed on the altar of authority and conjecture?

This had been the question around which Reid's thoughts were revolving in the twenty years preceding the publication of his book. 'For my own satisfaction,' he tells us, 'I entered into a serious examination of the principles upon which this sceptical system is built; and was not a little surprised to find that it leans with its whole weight upon a hypothesis which is ancient indeed, and hath been very generally received by philosophers, but of which I could find no solid proof. The hypothesis I mean is—that we do not really perceive things that are external, but only certain images and pictures of them imprinted upon the mind, which are called "impressions" and "ideas." I thought it unreasonable, upon the authority of philosophers, to admit an hypothesis which, in my opinion, overturns all philosophy, all religion and virtue, and all common sense; and I resolved to inquire into this subject anew, without regard to any hypothesis.'

To *accept* as a spiritual fact the judgment of human nature, which assures me that when I am seeing or touching I am 'face to face' with a reality that exists independently of my changing sensations or ideas, instead of trying in vain by reasoning to *prove* the existence of this reality by means of intervening sensations and ideas,—this was the alternative he adopted. I dismiss the unwarranted supposition that only my own mind and its invisible contents can be immediately manifested to me; and I fall back on the perception I have of something solid and extended, and therefore more and other than a mere sensation or idea, as what is present to me when I see and touch. Recognition of the fact that our five senses somehow bring us into a consciousness of what is neither a transitory sensation nor an idea of a sensation, but something independent of me, and that would continue to exist after I individually had ceased to exist—this recognition of external realities is Reid's key to sound philosophy. It is a displacement of the so-called 'ideas' of the philosophers, and of fallacious inferences founded upon them, and a substitution of the common reasonable sense, or common judgment of reason, which neither requires nor admits of logical proof. Reid might say that what is most worth proving cannot be logically proved. We all have a direct perception of external reality which cannot be eradicated by reasoning. Abolition of the prejudice which interposed *reasonings founded on unreal ideas* between our perception and the solid and extended reality, seemed to Reid, in virtue of its far-reaching consequences, to be the chief good he had as a philosopher secured to mankind. In his old age he writes thus to Dr. Gregory:—

'The merit of what you are pleased to call *my philosophy* lies, I think, chiefly in having called in question the common theory of ideas, or images of things in the mind, being the only objects of thought—a theory founded on natural prejudices, and so universally received as to be interwoven with the structure of language. Yet, were I to give you a detail of what led me to call in question this theory, after I had long held it as self-evident and unquestionable, you would think, as I do, that there was much of chance in the matter. The discovery was the birth of time, not of genius; and Berkeley and Hume did more to bring it to light than the man that hit upon it. I think there is hardly anything that can be called *mine* in the philosophy of mind which does not follow with ease from the detection of this prejudice.'

Yet Reid's *Inquiry* has been condemned as an unphilosophical appeal from the thoughtful to vulgar intelligence, making the unreflecting many supreme judges in questions intelligible only to the reflecting few. His employment of 'common sense' to express the regulative principle of his philosophy would put his book outside philosophical literature, if this term were taken as a synonym for unreasoned opinion—the average judgments of the man in the street. Reid's own account of what he means by common sense, not to speak of Hume's recognition of the 'deeply philosophical' character of the argument in the *Inquiry*, should protect him against this imputation. He describes the common sense to which he constantly appeals as 'the first degree of reason,' and as having for its office 'to judge of things self-evident.' As such, he contrasts it with reasoning, or 'the second degree of reason, which draws conclusions that are not self-evident from the self-evident judgments of the common sense.' This distinction between the common rational sense, on which a knowledge of the universe, like the human, which falls short of omniscience, *must* ultimately turn, and those judgments that are reached by logical reasoning, corresponds to what the Greeks distinguished as noetic and dianoetic power of reason in man. Reid's genuine judgments of the common sense may be regarded as the divinely inspired response to questions which can be determined for man only by this ideal man latent in us all—judgments verified by the insanity that is implied in resisting them in our actions.

As obtrusive examples of judgments of the common sense, Reid takes the logically undemonstrable convictions (1) of the existence of things external to and independent of me and my perceptions; (2) of my individual personal existence and continuous personal identity; and (3) of the uniformity, and therefore interpretability, of nature, implying that I may form conclusions about what I have not experienced by what I have experienced. I cannot demonstrate the truth of these judgments: I can only justify them in reason by showing that human nature responds to them, and forbids me to reject them in my actions, on pain of being judged a lunatic, whatever I may say in my speculative theories. 'Such original and natural judgments,' he says, 'are part of the furniture which *nature* hath given to the human understanding. They are the inspiration of the Almighty. They serve to direct us in the common affairs of life, when our reasoning faculty would leave us in the dark; they are part of our constitution; all the discoveries of our reason are grounded upon them; they make up what is called *the common sense* of mankind. A remarkable deviation from them, arising from a disorder in the constitution, is what we call *lunacy*, as when a man believes that he is made of glass. When a man suffers himself to be reasoned out of the principles of common sense by metaphysical arguments, we call it *metaphysical lunacy*, which differs from the other species of the distemper in this, that it is not continued, but intermittent; it is apt to seize the patient in solitary and speculative moments; but when he enters into sanity, Common Sense recovers her authority.'

It is the first of these three examples of the common sense that is the subject of the *Inquiry* — intended as preliminary to others which may follow. 'A clear enumeration and explication of the principles of common sense' was henceforward Reid's ultimate aim; but thus far he took those involved in our experience when we are tasting, or smelling, or hearing, or touching, or seeing. As axioms and definitions are the preliminaries of abstract mathematical reasonings, so our sensuous perceptions through the five senses are the preliminaries to reasonings about concrete realities in the world of change. The leading principle of the *Inquiry* is, that something extended, solid, and movable is directly manifested in our sensuous experiences, equally with the direct manifestations of our own sensations and other feelings when we are conscious of them; and also that we are obliged by common sense to regard extended, solid, and movable things as *other* than mere transitory sensation or idea. Extended things, large or small, refuse to be melted down into sensations or states of one's private consciousness. Take this specimen of philosophical argument for accepting perceptions which cannot be logically demonstrated, but which the common sense of human nature refuses to reject:—

'Suppose I am pricked with a pin, I ask, is the *pain* I feel a sensation? Undoubtedly it is. There can be nothing that resembles pain in an inanimate thing : the pain must be in me, a living being. But I ask again, is the *pin* a sensation? To this question I feel myself under a necessity of answering that the pin is not a sensation, nor can have the least resemblance to any sensation. The pin has length and thickness, figure and weight. A sensation can have none of these qualities. I am not more certain that the pain I feel *is* a sensation than that the pin *is not* a sensation. Yet the pin is an object of sense ; and I am as certain that I perceive its figure and hardness by my senses as that I feel pain when I am pricked by it.'

This is to say that if, with the philosophers, I *call* the pin as well as the pain a sensation or an idea, I must mean by 'sensation' and 'idea,' when I apply those words to the pin, not a private self-contained feeling or a fancy, in which I am only manifesting my conscious self, but (so to speak) a *public* sensation or idea—perceivable by other persons as well as by me—a manifestation, in short, of what is *outside my mind*—of something that exists permanently in *space* and not transitorily in *me*—and that is thus fit to be a medium of communication between me and other living persons, informing me of their existence and in some measure of their thoughts—all which (Reid takes for granted) each person's private feelings and fancies could not do. But to employ the words 'sensation' and 'idea' in this new meaning, and to speak of an idea as public or external, would be an abuse of language. We must mark, always by appropriate words, distinctions which we are obliged to acknowledge in fact. The inspirations or revelations of the common sense, in and through which the Almighty Power gives us an understanding of the life and world in which we find ourselves, inspirations in which all men are believed more or less to participate, require us to distinguish the solid and extended pin, as something public or outward, in contrast to the private feeling of pain, of which no one except the person who feels it is conscious. I am thus obliged to recognise more in existence than my own sensations and ideas—as much obliged as I am to recognise my sensations and ideas themselves when I am conscious of them. Only so can I find myself living in an environment that is capable of signifying the contemporaneous life, and some of the thoughts and feelings of other persons. In all this I am only falling back on the divine revelations of the common sense. They make me reject in conduct what is inconsistent with them; although this natural obligation is all the reason I can give in justification of my obedience.

It is thus that Reid recognises his right in reason to grasp realities that are independent of his individual self; and he thinks that he is doing this philosophically by getting rid of the unphilosophical supposition, that he needs to work his way to them by logical reasoning, founded on wholly inward impressions. The true philosophy of perception with him is to discharge the medium, and at once take the bull by the horns.

Some may think that the *Inquiry* represents wasted labour—that the 'metaphysical lunacy' which abolishes personal pronouns as meaningless words, and inconsistently reasons that all who reason must be fools, is at the best the idle intellectual pastime of persons who pretend to be universal sceptics—all which Reid has taken too seriously, and which at any rate by its self-contradiction refutes itself. For it asserts that assertion is impossible. It is an argument that concludes for the rejection of the postulates without which it is impossible for human beings to reason at all. It is a philosophy that destroys itself in destroying all philosophy. The suicide does not need to be put to death.

Yet the suicide, doubly slain in the *Inquiry*, may be used as a warning of the consequence of doing violence to the genuine common sense, or ideal man that is latent in each man; especially on subjects in which doubt is easier than in the case of outward things and persons. The 'metaphysical lunacy' of doubt about the existence of other persons may be acknowledged, while the common sense, unawake in its moral or spiritual elements, fails to protest against ethical atheism or agnosticism. What Reid calls the common sense is alive consciously in various degrees, in different persons, in different countries and periods. A common sense of the existence of outward things and persons is practically awake in all sane minds. But the spiritual convictions, of which some are hardly conscious, may be rejected even practically without obvious lunacy. And something is gained for those convictions, if it can be shown, as a *reductio ad absurdum*, that their rejection involves the moral sceptic too in the 'lunacy' of universal doubt and pessimist despair.

That Reid lays much stress on 'calling in question the common theory of ideas or images in perception' is explained by his assumption, that this theory involves perversion of the common sense even in its preliminary contact with outward things in sense, thus obviously discrediting it as the final court of appeal in every other instance. It may in this way be taken as a plea for a more faithful adherence on the part of philosophers to the genuine common-sense judgments, which can be made to respond to an adequate appeal, however dormant they may be in individuals. This final appeal to human nature must, in short, be to human nature *as it is in fact*, not to human nature *as distorted in hypothesis*.

For, after all, the root of the agnosticism which is found in history alternating with the final faith of the common sense, lies deeper than in mistaken hypotheses of philosophers about our perceptions in sense. Reid's substitution in philosophy of immediate for mediate perception of matter is therefore an inadequate cure. The periodically returning doubt concerns, not the outness or inwardness of what is revealed to sense, but the meaning and character of the Power that is at work within the universe of matter and mind, and with which we first come into contact and collision in sense. Is it, in its final and pervading Power, a bad or a good sort of universe that we open our eyes upon, when we begin to exercise our senses? What are its final relations to me, and my final relations to it? Nobody doubts the existence of things and persons, so far as they are revealed to the senses. But what is our implied Common Sense of the final meaning of the Whole? Am I to put an optimist or a pessimist ultimate interpretation upon it all? The lurid mixture of pain and pleasure, evil and good, presented by the animated world, combined with spiritually dormant common sense in individual men,—is surely a more potent factor of agnostic doubt than an erroneous account of perception in circulation among persons who speculate.

Reid's course of thought amidst new surroundings in Glasgow brought him nearer to the source and corrective of the scepticism that is aroused by the suspicious-looking universe of mingled good and evil, to which our sense perceptions introduce us.

CHAPTER VI

GLASGOW COLLEGE: THE PROFESSOR OF
MORAL PHILOSOPHY

1764—1780

IN November 1764 we find Reid, now almost fifty-five years of age, in the Chair of Moral Philosophy in the Old College in the High Street of Glasgow. The Reid family lived then, and for two years after, not in the Professors' Court within the College, but a quarter of a mile away, in an old-fashioned street called the Drygate.[1] The manuscript in the family bible records that Reid was admitted to the Glasgow professorship on the 12th of June. He carried with him from the quaint manse in Aberdeen to his new home in the Drygate, his wife, three daughters, all above twenty years of age, and two boys; they left three infant children buried in Aberdeenshire. The Glasgow Chair supplied an income, including fees, somewhat in advance of the Aberdeen regency; and its duties required concentrated study of intellectual and moral agency in man, instead of the dispersion over a wide range of the phenomena and laws of matter and mind which was necessary in King's College. Yet it was 'not without reluctance,' we are told, that he consented to tear himself from a spot where he had so long been fastening his roots; and much as he loved the society in which he passed the remainder of his days, the advantages

[1] Between the College and the Cathedral, diverging to the east.

of the change hardly compensated for the sacrifice of feeling caused by the break in his early habits and associations.

Glasgow in 1898 is even more changed from Glasgow in 1764 than Aberdeen when Reid lived in it from Aberdeen as it is now. To-day Glasgow is the second city in Britain, with nearly a million of people, the industrial metropolis of the north, with all the stir of industrial life. It was then a provincial town with hardly thirty thousand inhabitants, almost inaccessible from the sea, surrounded by the cornfields and hedgerows and orchards of Lanarkshire, its few streets converging on the Cathedral and the College with their historic associations. 'Glasgow,' according to *Humphrey Clinker*, 'is the pride of Scotland. It is one of the prettiest towns in Europe.' Pennant describes it as 'the best built of any second-rate city I ever saw. The view from the Cross has an air of vast magnificence.' In 1764 it was only laying the foundations of its present commercial fame. The tobacco trade with the American plantations, and the sugar trade with the West Indies, had hardly altered its character as an ancient Church and University town. 'Jupiter Carlyle,' referring to Glasgow before the middle of last century, speaks of 'a few families of ancient citizens who pretended to be gentlemen; and a few others, recently settled, who had obtained wealth and consideration in trade. The rest were shopkeepers and mechanics, who occupied large warerooms to furnish cargoes to Virginia. It was then usual for the sons of merchants to attend the College for one or two years, and a few of them completed their academical education.'

The College in the High Street, erected early in the seventeenth century, seemed to Samuel Johnson in 1773 'without a sufficient share in the magnificence of the place.' Nevertheless he found 'learning an object of wide importance, and the habit of application much more general than in the neighbouring University of Edinburgh.' The two College squares, connected with memories of many generations in the west of Scotland, have been likened to those of Lincoln College in Oxford. About the middle of last century from three to four hundred students gathered in those curious old courts, almost all living in apartments in the town, a few boarded in the houses of professors. They wore scarlet gowns, 'most of which,' when Wesley visited Glasgow, 'were very dirty, some very ragged, and all of very coarse cloth.' The houses of the professors formed a square on the north side of the College, built early in the eighteenth century. Eastward were the College gardens and the park, through which the classic Molendinar found its way to the Clyde. It was a quaint and curious old-world life that was then lived in the College, and in the High Street, passing from the College to the Cathedral at one end and from the College to the Cross at the other.

In the half-century before Reid was admitted to his Glasgow Chair, the University had professors of more than Scottish reputation. Glasgow is in fact associated with almost all the names that adorn the literature of Philosophy in Scotland in the last century and in this. Adam Smith was Reid's immediate predecessor in the Chair of Morals. His *Theory of Moral Sentiments* had been for five years before the world when he resigned his professorship to give to literature what Sir James Mackintosh describes as 'perhaps the only book which produced an immediate, general, and irrevocable change in some of the most important parts of the legislation of all civilised states '—fit to be ranked with the classic works of Grotius, Locke, and

Montesquieu—its author 'the first economical philosopher, and perhaps the most eloquent theoretical moralist, of modern times.' Smith's predecessor was Francis Hutcheson, author of that *Inquiry into our Ideas of Beauty and Virtue* which gave rise to Reid's New Machar essay on 'Quantity' in 1748, the reputed father of modern philosophy in Scotland;—and in the second quarter of last century the most potent agent and pioneer of the liberal culture and literary taste which made the intellectual moderation of the eighteenth century in Scotland so remarkable a contrast to the less tolerant spiritual fervour of the seventeenth. This influence was continued by his friend and biographer, William Leechman, the Principal of Glasgow College in 1764, still remembered as one of the philosophical theologians of the Church of Scotland. 'It was owing to Hutcheson and Leechman,' says Carlyle, 'that a new school was formed in the western provinces of Scotland, where the clergy till that period were narrow and bigoted, and had never ventured to range their minds beyond the bounds of strict orthodoxy. For though neither of these professors taught any heresy, yet they opened and enlarged the minds of the students, which soon gave them a turn for inquiry; the result of which was candour and liberality of sentiment. From experience this freedom of thought was not found so dangerous as might at first be apprehended; for though the more daring youth at first made excursions into the unbounded regions of metaphysical perplexity, yet all the more judicious soon returned to the lower sphere of long-established truths, which they found not only more subservient to the good order of society, but necessary to fix their own minds in some degree of stability.' Gershom Carmichael, too, is not to be forgotten.

He was Hutcheson's predecessor, with an intellectual and religious influence not inconsiderable in the opening years of last century, author of a Latin manual of logic which appeared in 1720, and a *Synopsis Theologiæ Naturalis*, published shortly before his death in 1729, but best known perhaps as editor of Puffendorff.

Reid thus entered Glasgow College when it was the centre of the reviving philosophical and literary activity of Scotland in the modern spirit. He met colleagues and fellow-citizens who were in sympathy with his own sincere and independent scientific temper. The aged Simpson, restorer of ancient geometry, who had lately retired from the mathematical chair, which he had adorned for half a century, was a congenial mathematician of European fame. Joseph Black, the most celebrated British chemist of his generation, was illustrating his own discoveries in his College lectures, and drawing the attention of the world to the phenomena of latent heat. The vigour and acuteness of Millar were educating a new generation in jurisprudence and statesmanship. Moore, the author of *Zeluco*, an eminent Glasgow physician, was adding to its literary name. The grandfather, and afterwards the father, of Sir William Hamilton held in succession the Chair of Anatomy, both colleagues of Reid, who might have been seen in the College Courts when his future editor and commentator was there in his infancy.

Reid's inaugural lecture as Professor of Moral Philosophy, delivered on the 10th of October 1764, is among his unpublished manuscripts at Birkwood. The opening sentences (deleted as irrelevant in after years) are not without interest in the characteristic modesty and candour of the reference to Adam Smith, his predecessor:—

'Before entering upon the subject of my prelections, there are some things which I think proper to lay before you, and to which I beg your attention. I doubt not that you are all sensible of the loss which the University, and you in particular, sustain by the resignation of the learned and ingenious gentleman who last filled this chair. Those who knew him most and had most access to attend his prelections, and especially those who most profited by them, will be most sensible of their loss. I had not the happiness of his personal acquaintance, for want of opportunity; though I wished for it, and now wish for it far more than ever. But I could not be a stranger to his fame and reputation, nor to the respect with which his lectures from this chair were heard by a very crowded audience. I am much a stranger to his system, unless so far as he hath published it to the world. But a man of so great genius and penetration must have struck new light to the subjects which he treated, as well as have handled them in an excellent and instructive manner. I shall be much obliged to any of you, gentlemen, or to any others, who can furnish me with notes of his prelections, whether in morals, jurisprudence, politics, or rhetorick. I shall always be desirous to borrow light from every quarter, and to adopt what appears to me sound and solid in every system, and ready to change my opinions upon conviction, or to change my method and materials where I can do it to advantage. I desire to live no longer than this candour and ingenuity, this openness of mind to education and information, live with me.'

An apology follows for the imperfect preparation of a first course, inadequately provided for by the miscellaneous lectures in physics and metaphysics at Aberdeen. The past performance of Adam Smith, and the high expectation associated with the new professor, the author of the *Inquiry*, were doubtless fresh in the minds of the crowded audience that met on that October morning in the faint light of the Old College class-room. The audience, the new professor, and his predecessor, have all now receded into the dim distance, and are seen under the cold light of history. The lectures delivered in the years that followed are preserved at Birkwood, in Reid's valley of the Dee— lectures on Pneumatology, Ethics, Jurisprudence, and Political Philosophy—for the most part embodied in substance in the published *Essays* of his old age.

Reid's placid temperament and restrained imagination suggest sober unadorned statement, and cautious inference founded on fact, not fervid eloquence, as the character of his prelections. He was more likely slowly to influence opinion by his books than to startle a youthful audience by spoken words. This conjecture is confirmed by the account of Reid in the Glasgow class-room given by Dugald Stewart, who was among his students in 1772-73. 'In his elocution and mode of instruction,' Stewart says, 'there was nothing peculiarly attractive. He seldom if ever indulged in the warmth of extempore discourse; nor was his manner of reading calculated to increase the effect of what he had committed to writing. Such, however, was the simplicity and perspicuity of his style, such the gravity and authority of his character, and such the general interest of his young hearers in the doctrines which he taught, that by the numerous audiences to which his instructions were addressed he was heard uniformly with the most silent and respectful attention.' And this delivery of deep and patient thought, regarding the duties and relations of man, and the foundation of his beliefs, was continued in the class-room for sixteen years.

As we might expect from their mental affinities, Reid greatly esteemed the works of Bishop Butler. Among the manuscripts at Birkwood is an abstract of the *Analogy*; and Butler's ethical writings were recommended to his students as the best in the literature of moral philosophy, with regret to see them superseded in England by the productions of inferior moralists. In tone and method of inquiry Reid is the Butler of Scotland. And Butler, too, is the Reid of England in his trustful appeals to what Reid would call the common sense. When Butler asks himself whether we may not be deceived in our natural sense of our continuous personal identity, he replies, that 'this question may be asked at the end of any demonstration; because it is a question concerning the truth of perception by memory. And he who can doubt whether perception by memory can in this case be depended on, may doubt also whether perception by reasoning, or indeed whether any intuitive perception, can. Here then we can go no further. For it is ridiculous to attempt to *prove* the truth of those perceptions, whose truth we can no otherwise prove than by other perceptions which there is just the same ground to suspect; or to attempt to prove the truth of our faculties, which can no otherwise be proved than by these very suspected faculties themselves.' This is the substance of the argument that rests on the data of the sense or reason with which human nature is inspired.

Reid's homely letters to his Aberdeen friends, Andrew and David Skene, give some interesting pictures of the details of the family's life, in the years which immediately followed the settlement in Glasgow. The extracts that follow may help the reader to form the pictures.

In a letter to Dr. Andrew Skene, dated November 15, 1764, we see the Moral Philosophy class-room on a winter morning a hundred and thirty years ago, and life in the Drygate home a few weeks after the family entered it:—

'I must launch forth in the morning, so as to be at the College (which is a walk of eight minutes) half an hour after seven, when I speak for an hour without interruption to an audience of about a hundred. At eleven I examine for an hour upon my morning prelection; but my audience is a little more than a third part of what it was in the morning. In a week or two I must, for three days in the week, have a second prelection at twelve, upon a different subject, where my audience will be made up of those who hear me in the morning but do not attend at eleven. My hearers commonly attend my class two years at least. They pay fees for the first two years, and then they are *cives* of the class, and may attend gratis as many years as they please. Many attend the moral philosophy class four or five years; so that I have many preachers and students of divinity and law of considerable standing, before whom I stand in awe to speak without more preparation than I have leisure for. I have a great inclination to attend some of the professors here, several of whom are very eminent in their way; but I cannot find leisure. Much time is consumed in our college meetings about business, of which we have commonly four or five in the week. We have a Literary Society once a week, consisting of the Masters and two or three more; where each of the members has a discourse once in the session. . . . Near a third part of our students are Irish. Thirty came over lately in one ship, besides three that went to Edinburgh. We have a good many English, and some foreigners. Many of the Irish, as well as Scotch, are poor, and come up late to save money; so that we are not yet fully convened, although I have been teaching ever since the 10th of October. Those who pretend to know, say that the number of students this year, when fully convened, will amount to 300. . . . By this time I am sure you have enough of the College; for you know as much as I can tell you of the fine houses of the Masters, of the Astronomical Observatory, of Robin Foulis' collection of pictures and painting college, and of the foundry for types and printing-house. Therefore I will carry you home to my own house, which lyes among the middle of the weavers, like the back-wynd in Aberdeen. You go through a long, dark, abominably nasty entry, which leads you into a clean little close. You walk upstairs to a neat little dining-room, and find as many other little rooms as just accommodate my family; so scantily that my apartment is a closet of six feet by eight or nine off the dining-room. To balance these little inconveniences, the house is new and free of buggs; it has the best air and finest prospect in Glasgow; the privilege of a large garden, very airy, to walk in, which is not so nicely kept, but one may use freedom with it. A five minutes' walk leads us up a rocky precipice into a large park, partly planted with firs, and partly open, which overlooks the town and all the country round, and gives a view of the windings of the Clyde for a great way. The ancient Cathedral stands at the foot of the rock, half of its height below you, and half above you; and indeed it is a very magnificent pile. When we came here, the street we live in (which is called the Drygate) was infested with the small-pox, which were very mortal. Two families in our neighbourhood lost all their children, being three each. Little David was seized with the infection, and had a very great eruption both on his face and over his whole body, which you will believe would discompose his mother. . . . Although my salary here be the same as Aberdeen, yet if the class does not fall off, nor my health, so as to disable me from teaching, I believe I shall be able to live as easily as at Aberdeen, notwithstanding the differences in the expense of living at the two places. I have touched about £70 of fees, and may possibly make out the £100 this session... The common people here have a gloom in their countenance, which I am at a loss whether to ascribe to their religion or to the air and climate. There is certainly more of religion among the common people in this town than in Aberdeen; and although it has a gloomy enthusiastical cast, yet I think it makes them tame and sober. I have not heard either of a house or of a head broke, or of a pocket picked, or of any flagrant crime, since I came here. I have not heard any swearing in the streets, nor seen a man drunk (excepting, *inter nos*, one Prof—r) since I came here. . . . If this scroll tire you, impute it to this, that to-morrow is to be employed in choosing a Rector, and I can sleep till ten o'clock, which I shall not do again for six weeks.'

After the first winter, and when he had gained some experience of Glasgow, he writes to Dr. David Skene, on 13th July 1765:—

'I have a strong inclination to attend the chymical lecture the next winter; but am afraid I shall not have time. I have

had but very imperfect hints of Dr. Black's theory of fire. . . .
Chemistry seems to be the only branch of philosophy that can
be said to be in a progressive state here, although other
branches are neither ill taught nor ill studied. I never considered Dolland's telescopes till I came here. I think they
open a new field in optics which may greatly enrich that part
of philosophy. . . . I find a variety of things here to amuse me
in the literary world, and want nothing so much as my old
friends, whose place I cannot expect at my time of life to
supply. I think the common people here and in the neighbourhood greatly inferior to the common people with you.
They are Bœotian in their understandings, fanatical in their
religion, and clownish in their dress and manners. The clergy
encourage this fanaticism too much, and find it the only way
to popularity. I often hear a gospel here which you know
nothing about; for you neither hear it from the pulpit nor will
you find it in the Bible. What is your Philosophical Society
doing? Still battling about D. Hume? or have you time to
look in? . . . I believe you do not like to be charged with
compliments, otherwise I would desire of you to remember me
respectfully to Sir Archibald Grant, Sir Arthur and Lady
Forbes, and others of my country acquaintances, when you
have occasion to see them.'

In another letter to Dr. David, written about Christmas
in his second winter, we find that—

'Mr. Watt has made two small improvements in the steam-engine.[1] [These are minutely described.] . . . I have attended
Dr. Black's lectures. His doctrine of latent heat is the only
thing I have yet heard that is altogether new. And indeed I
look upon it as a very great discovery. . . . I have not met
with any botanists here. Our College is considerably more
crowded than it was last session. My class indeed is much the
same as last year, but all the rest are better. I believe the
number of our students of one kind or another may be between
four and five hundred. But the College at Edinburgh is increased this year much more than we are. The Moral Philosophy class there is more than double ours. The Professor,

[1] Watt began those experiments in Glasgow about 1763.

Ferguson, is indeed, as far as I can judge, a man of a noble spirit, of very elegant manners, and has an uncommon flow of eloquence. I hear he is about to publish, I don't know under what title, a natural history of man; exhibiting a view of him in the savage state, and in the several successive states of pasturage, agriculture, and commerce. Our Society [Senate] is not so harmonious as I wish. Schemes of interest, pushed by some and opposed by others, are like to divide us into parties, and perhaps engage us in law suits. Mrs. Reid, Pegie, and I, have all had a severe cold and cough. I have been keeping the house these two days in order to get the better of it.'

On 'December 30th, 1765,' a less sanguine view appears, in a letter to Andrew Skene:—

'I assure you I can rarely find an hour which I am at liberty to dispose of as I please. The most disagreeable thing in the teaching part is to have a great number of stupid Irish teagues, who attend classes for two or three years to qualify them for teaching schools or being dissenting teachers. I preach to them as St. Francis did to the fishes. I don't know what pleasure he had in his audience; but I should have none in mine, if there were not in it a mixture of reasonable creatures. I confess I think there is a smaller proportion of these in my class this year than there was the last. I have long been of the opinion that, in a right constituted College, there ought to be two professors for each class—one for the dunces, and another for those who have parts. The province of the former would not be the most agreeable, but perhaps it would require the greatest talents, and therefore ought to be accounted the post of honour. There is no part of my time more disagreeably spent than that which is spent in college meetings; and I should have been attending one at this moment if a bad cold I have got had not furnished me with an excuse. These meetings are become more disagreeable by an evil spirit of party that seems to put us in a ferment, and I am afraid will produce bad consequences. The temper of our northern Colonies makes mercantile people here look very grave. It is said that the effects in these colonies belonging to this town amount to above

£400,000.[1] The mercantile people are for suspending the Stamp-act, and redressing the grievances of the colonists. . . . In what light the House of Commons will view this matter I don't know, but it seems to me one of the most important matters that have come before them. I wish often an evening with you, such as we have enjoyed in the days of former times, to settle the important affairs of Church and State, of Colleges and Corporations. I have found this the best expedient to think of them without melancholy and chagrin. And I think all that a man has to do in the world is to keep his temper and to do his duty. Mrs. Reid is tolerably well just now, but is often ailing.'

In a letter to Dr. David, in March 1766, he refers to the death of his early friend, John Stewart, the Mathematical Professor in Marischal College, and his companion in the English tour thirty years before:—

'Mr. Stewart's death affects me deeply. A sincere friendship, begun at twelve years of age, and continued to my time of life, without any interruption, cannot but give some pangs. You know his worth; yet it was shaded ever since you knew him by too great abstraction from the world. The former part of his life was more amiable and more social; but the whole was of a piece in virtue, candour, and humanity. . . . I have always regarded him as my best tutor, though of the same age with me. If the giddy part of my life was in any degree spent innocently and virtuously, I owe it to him more than to any human creature; for I could not but be virtuous in his company, and I could not be so happy in any other. But I must leave this pleasing melancholy subject. He is happy; and I shall often be happy in the remembrance of our friendship; and I hope we shall meet again.'

A minute account of Black's theory of latent heat follows.

Later in the same year, Black was called to the Chair of Chemistry in Edinburgh, which he filled for nearly thirty

[1] The American revolt was a severe stroke to Glasgow at the time, though it led to a great development of manufactures in the city afterwards. See Colville's *By-Ways of History* (1897), pp. 281-314.

years, and in Reid's letters to the Skenes there is much about candidates for the vacant office in Glasgow, with a suggestion that David Skene should himself enter the lists. 'There is a great spirit of inquiry among the young people here. Literary merit is much regarded; and I conceive the opportunities a man has of improving himself are much greater here than at Aberdeen. The communication with Edinburgh is easy. One goes in the stage coach to Edinburgh before dinner; has all the afternoon there, and returns to dinner at Glasgow next day; so that if you have any ambition to get into the College of Edinburgh (which I think you ought to have), I conceive Glasgow would be a good step.'

The appeal was ineffectual. Meantime his own appointment, as an 'examinator' of candidates for the vacant Mathematical Chair in Marischal College, made a visit to Aberdeen necessary, as anticipated in a letter on 'May 8th':—

'My class will be over in less than a month, and by that time I shall be glad to have some respite. I hope to have the pleasure of seeing my friends in Aberdeen in August, if not sooner. We have had a stronger College this year than ever before. We have been remarkably free from riots and disorders among the students; and I did not indeed expect that 350 young fellows could have keen kept quiet for so many months with so little trouble. . . . You'll say to all this that cadgers are aye speaking of crooksaddles. I think so they ought; besides, I have nothing else to say to you, and have had no time to think of anything but my crooksaddles for seven months past. When the session's over, I must rub up my mathematics against the month of August. There is one candidate for your profession of mathematics to go from this College; and if your College get a better man, or a better mathematician, they will be very lucky.[1] I am so sensible of the honour the Magistrates

---

[1] William Traill, a Glasgow graduate, was elected. Playfair (of St. Andrews), afterwards Professor John Playfair of Edinburgh, was also a candidate, then only eighteen.

have done me in naming me to be one of the examinators, that I will not decline it, though I confess I like the honour better than the office.'

In the autumn of 1766 Reid exchanged the house in the Drygate for an official residence in the Professors' Court of the Old College. This appears in a letter to Dr. Andrew Skene on December 17th:—

'I live now in the College, and have no distance to walk to my class in dark mornings, as I had before. I enjoy this ease, though I am not sure whether the necessity of walking up and down a steep hill[1] three or four times a day was not of use. I have of late had a little of your distemper, finding a giddiness in my head when I lie down, or rise, or turn myself in my bed. Our College is very well peopled this session. My public class is above three score, besides the private class. Dr. Smith never had so many in one year. There is nothing so uneasy to me here as our factions in the College.'

In February 1767, along with other local news, we find this in a letter to David Skene:—

'We are now resolved to have a canal from Carron to this place, if the Parliament allows it. £40,000 was subscribed last week by the merchants of the Carron Company for this purpose.[2] Our medical college has fallen off greatly this session, most of the students of medicine having followed Dr. Black to Edinburgh. The natural and moral philosophy classes are more numerous than they have ever been; but I expect a great falling off, if I see another session. I was just now seeing your furnace along with Dr. Irvine. . . . If I could find a machine as proper for analysing ideas, moral sentiments, and other materials belonging to the fourth kingdom, I believe I should find in my heart to bestow the money first. I have the more use for a machine of this kind, because my alembic for performing these operations—I mean my cranium—has been a little out of order this winter, by a vertigo, which has made

[1] The Bell of the Brae.
[2] The Forth and Clyde Canal was commenced in 1768 and opened from sea to sea in 1790.

my studies go on heavily, though it has not hitherto interrupted my teaching. I have found air and exercise and a clean stomach the best remedies; but I cannot command the two former as often as I could wish. I am sensible that the air of a crowded class is bad, and often thought of carrying my class to the Common Hall; but I was afraid it might have been construed as a piece of ostentation.'

Reid's letter of condolence to Dr. David Skene on the death of his father, in September 1767, mentions the loss of his own infant daughter, 'my sweet little Bess,' and also refers to an excursion to Hamilton 'with Mr. Beattie'— the only occasion on which, for more than three months, he had been more than three miles from Glasgow. 'Having time at command,' he had been tempted 'to fall to the tumbling over books; as we have a vast number here which I had not access to see at Aberdeen. But this is a *mare magnum*, wherein one is tempted by hopes of discoveries to make a tedious voyage, which seldom repays the labour. I have long ago found my memory to be like a vessel that is full: if you pour in more, you lose as much as you gain; and on this account I have a thousand times resolved to give up all pretence to what is called learning, being satisfied that it is more profitable to ruminate on the little I have laid up than to add to the indigested heap. I have had little society, the College people being out of town, and have almost lost the faculty of speaking by disuse. I blame myself for having corresponded so little with my friends at Aberdeen. I wished to try Lumsden's experiment which you was so good as to communicate to me. . . . A nasty custom I have of chewing tobacco has been the reason of my observing a species of as nasty little animals. I spit in a basin of sawdust, which, when it comes to be drenched, produces a vast number of animals, three or four times as large as a louse, and not very different in shape; but armed with four or five rows of prickles like a hedgehog, which seem to serve it as feet. Its motion is very sluggish. It lies drenched in the aforesaid mass, which swarms with these animals of all ages from top to bottom. . . . I have gone over Sir James Stewart's great book of political economy, wherein I think there is a great deal of good material—carelessly put together indeed; but I think it contains more sound principles concerning commerce and police than any book we have yet had. We had the favour of a visit from Sir Archibald Grant. It gave me much pleasure to see him retain his spirits and vigour.' A letter in October mentions that Reid had 'passed eight days lately with Lord Kames at Blair-Drummond,' and that his lordship is preparing a fourth edition of his *Elements*. He adds, 'I have been labouring at *Barbara Celarent* for three weeks bygone.' A new friend, Lord Kames, here comes in sight.

The last of the Skene letters is dated three years later, in 1770. After pressing David Skene to visit him in Glasgow, he ends thus:—'As to myself, the immaterial world has swallowed up all my thoughts since I came here; but I meet with few that have travelled far in that region, and am often left to pursue my dreary way in a more solitary manner than when we used to meet at the Club.'

The homely simplicity of Reid's character is shown in those letters. They differ from the letters we have after the Skenes disappear. These are almost all on questions in philosophy, and show a slow but steady advance in reflection upon the 'common sense' constitution of man's knowledge of the universe of matter and mind.

In 1772 there was sorrow in the Reid household. The

two eldest daughters, Jane and Margaret, both died, in the bloom of youth, leaving only the third daughter, Martha, who not long after married Dr. Patrick Carmichael, a Glasgow physician, and youngest son of Professor Gershom Carmichael. This marriage added much to the comfort of Reid's later years.

We have a passing glimpse of Reid in 1773, when he was entertained in Glasgow by Johnson and Boswell, at the *Saracen's Head Inn*, in the Gallowgate, 'that paragon of inns in the eyes of the Scotch, but wretchedly managed.' The travellers arrived there on the 28th of October, on their return from their romantic excursion to the Western Highlands. At the *Saracen's Head*, on the following morning, as Boswell tells us, 'Dr. Reid, the philosopher, and two other Glasgow professors, breakfasted with us,' and they met them afterwards at supper. 'I was not much pleased with any of them,' the sage wrote to Mrs. Thrale. 'The general impression upon my memory,' Boswell says, 'is, that we had not much conversation at Glasgow, where the professors, like their brethren at Aberdeen, did not venture to expose themselves much to the battery of cannon which they knew might play upon them.' It is a pity that Boswell's indifference, or indolence, on this occasion has deprived us of talk at the *Saracen's Head* and in the College Court, as dramatic in its way as the pictures of Rasay or Inch Kenneth. Notwithstanding Reid's cautious and modest silence, or want of vivacity, he surely said and heard something at those Glasgow breakfasts and suppers.

Before death had put an end to the letters to the Skenes, Reid had become intimate with one of the most notable men of the time in Scotland. I do not know how the intimacy began, but as early as 1767 we have found him referring to a visit to Lord Kames at Blair-Drummond, and to the mysteries of *Barbara Celarent*. This means that he was at work on the *Brief Account of Aristotle's Logic, with Remarks*, published seven years afterwards as an Appendix to one of Lord Kames' *Sketches of the History of Man*. The *Sketches* appeared in two quarto volumes, in 1774, and the *Brief Account* fills about seventy pages in the second volume. It was Reid's only appearance in print in the sixteen years of his public professorship in Glasgow. This, along with the essay on Quantity, given to the Royal Society in 1748, and the *Inquiry*, in 1764, made up his work as an author, until after he had ceased to be an oral teacher.

In Henry Home, Lord Kames, notwithstanding a temperament very different from his own, Reid found congenial companionship—a strong disposition to metaphysical speculation, a ready and accomplished if not deeply learned lawyer, and a considerable author. Kames was fourteen years his senior. Curiously, Henry Home's closest early friendship was with David Hume. Thirty years before his friendship with Reid, he advised Hume about the *Treatise of Human Nature*, and had given the youth an introduction to Bishop Butler. 'My opinions,' David writes in 1737, 'are so new, and even some terms I am obliged to make use of, that I could not propose, by any abridgment, to give my system an air of likelihood, or even to make it intelligible. I have had a greater desire of communicating to you a plan of the whole, that I believe it will not appear in public before the beginning of next winter. I am at present castrating my work, that is, cutting off its nobler parts, that is, endeavouring it shall give as little offence as possible. This is a piece of cowardice for which I blame myself. But I resolved not to be an enthusiast in philosophy while I was blaming other enthusiasms.' It was thus that Hume wrote about the book which, even in its 'castrated' form, startled Reid in the manse at New Machar, and determined his whole intellectual life. In 1751 Home published *Essays on the Principles of Morality and Natural Religion*, on which Jonathan Edwards congratulated him in a letter to Dr. Erskine. Yet his speculations, and his association with the sceptic, raised a suspicion of his orthodoxy in the General Assembly.

According to Lord Woodhouselee, his biographer, 'the intercourse of Lord Kames was frequent with his much-valued friend Dr. Reid, and they corresponded on various topics of philosophy—a correspondence which, notwithstanding the dissimilarity of character in many respects between these two eminent men, subsisted for a long period of years, with the most perfect cordiality and mutual esteem.' Dr. Reid, Dugald Stewart tells us, lived in the most cordial and affectionate friendship with Lord Kames, notwithstanding the avowed opposition of their sentiments on some moral questions to which he attached the highest importance. Both of them, however, were the friends of virtue and of mankind; and both were able to temper the warmth of free discussion with the forbearance and good humour founded on mutual esteem. 'No two men,' Stewart adds, 'ever exhibited a more striking contrast in their conversation or in their constitutional tempers—the one slow and cautious in his decisions, even on those topics which he had most diligently studied; reserved and silent in promiscuous society, and retaining, after all his literary eminence, the same simple and unassuming manners which he had brought from his country residence; the other, lively, rapid, and communicative; accustomed by his professional pursuits to wield with address the weapons of controversy, and not averse to a trial of his powers on questions the most foreign to his ordinary habits of inquiry. But these characteristical differences, while to their common friends they lent an additional charm to the distinguishing merits of each, served only to enliven their social intercourse, and to cement their mutual attachment.' From 1767 till the death of Lord Kames in December 1782, their intercourse was unbroken.[1]

Lord Kames thus explains Reid's contribution to the *Sketches* :—' In reviewing the foregoing Sketch, it occurred to me that a fair analysis of Aristotle's logic would be a valuable addition to the historical branch. A distinct and candid account of a system that for so many ages governed the reasoning part of mankind cannot but be acceptable to the public. Curiosity will be gratified in seeing a phantom delineated that so long fascinated the learned world; a phantom which, like the pyramids of Egypt, or hanging gardens of Babylon, is a structure of infinite genius, but absolutely useless, unless for raising wonder. Dr. Reid, Professor of Moral Philosophy in the College of Glasgow, relished the thought, and his friendship to me prevailed on him, after much solicitation, to undertake the laborious task. No man is better acquainted with Aristotle's writings; and (without any enthusiastic attachment) he holds that philosopher to be a first-rate genius.'

[1] Ramsay of Ochtertyre, who often met him at Blair Drummond, mentions that 'for more than fifteen years Reid spent great part of the College vacation there with Lord Kames.'

Measured by the present standard of Aristotelian criticism, Reid's exposition of the Organon, and estimate of its place in the development of human understanding, may seem meagre and inadequate; especially as the issue of seven years of preparation, and as his solitary contribution to philosophy in these sixteen years. But when we remember that Aristotelian logic was then under an eclipse, especially in Scotland, and that Reid's 'Brief Account' was an attempt to draw the Organon out of the obscurity to which it had been condemned by leaders of modern thought, the merit of his sober and sagacious commentary may be more recognised. It is as a signal monument of abstracted intellectual activity, rather than as a philosophical instrument for advancing or organising our knowledge, that Reid regards the syllogistic logic. He concludes that the art of syllogism is better fitted to promote scholastic litigation than real improvement in the sciences; he sees in it only 'a venerable piece of antiquity and a great effort of human genius.' When he contrasts the utility of Bacon's *Organum*, as a factor in the progressive intelligence of mankind, he fails to see that each Organon may consistently supplement the other.

Reid characteristically ends his account of the old Organon by suggesting an Organon, different from either the old or the new, as still wanting. This should neither, like Aristotle's, unfold only abstract forms of deductive reasoning, nor, like Bacon's, only methods for verifying inductive generalisations. It should be concerned with the rational principles which compose the Common Sense of mankind. 'All the real knowledge of mankind may be divided into two parts: the first consists of self-evident propositions, the second of those which are deduced by just reasoning from self-evident propositions. The line that divides these two ought to be marked as distinctly as possible, and principles that are really self-evident reduced to general axioms. Although first principles do not admit of direct proof, yet there must be certain marks by which those that are truly such may be distinguished from counterfeits. These marks ought to be described and applied to distinguish the genuine from the spurious. . . . This is a subject of such importance that if inquisitive men can be brought to the same unanimity in the first principles of the other sciences as in those of mathematics and natural philosophy, this might be considered as a third grand era in the progress of human reason.' Thus in 1774 Reid's thought still converges on the subject which had engaged him since the *Treatise of Human Nature* found its way into the manse of New Machar. Perhaps he was unduly sanguine in expecting unanimity regarding the ingredients of the final reason of mankind—so imperfectly developed in the individual consciousness, in its higher elements, as long as men are disposed to resist the final venture of the heart and conscience in their interpretation of the world and of human life.

It was in 1774 that Reid's appeal in 1764 to the common reason of human nature aroused hostile criticism. He had been seconded by others in his response to the sceptics. The resort to a 'sense' of self-evident truth, in his *Inquiry* in 1764, which itself looked like a reply to argument by feeling, was followed in 1766 by *An Appeal to Common Sense on behalf of Religion*, by Dr. James Oswald, minister of Methven in Perthshire. In 1770 Beattie's *Essay on the Nature and Immutability of Truth, in opposition to Sophistry and Scepticism*, followed. Oswald and Beattie were not deep and patient thinkers like Reid;[1] but the rising literary and social reputation of Beattie, secured for the *Essay on Truth* more rapid and widespread admiration than was given to the *Inquiry*. Beattie often visited London, was there one of the lions of the day, was made a D.C.L. of Oxford, and had interviews with George the Third, who admired his book, conferred a pension on Beattie, and rallied Mr. Dundas about 'Scotch Philosophy.' Reid, Beattie, and Oswald thus became known as a triumvirate of 'Scottish Philosophers'; and the appeal to common sense, in which they were at least verbally agreed, began to be spoken about as 'the Scottish Philosophy,' a term which has since been adopted in this country and abroad.

This Scottish triumvirate, helped into vogue by Beattie, roused Joseph Priestley, an English dissenter. Priestley had abandoned the Calvinism of his early creed for materialism, philosophical necessity, and free thought, and, after serving for some years as pastor of a nonconformist chapel in Cheshire, and next as a schoolmaster much devoted to experiments in the natural sciences, was already known as an author in natural science. In 1774, when he was living with Lord Shelburne, as librarian and literary companion, he appeared for the first time as a metaphysical critic, in *An Examination of Reid's Inquiry, Beattie's Essay, and Oswald's Appeal to Common Sense*. He played upon the term 'common sense,' and took for granted that the aim of the triumvirate was to substitute mere feeling and authority for reason,—the authority of the multitude for that of the

---

[1] Kant's uncritical identification of Reid's philosophical appeal to the common rational sense with the popular appeal and declamation of Oswald and even Beattie, is exposed by Professor Sidgwick in *Mind* (April 1895).

philosophical elect,—alleging blind instinct when unable to produce argument, and multiplying instincts to suit each controversial emergency. 'As men have imagined innate ideas, because they had forgot how they came by their ideas, the Scottish philosophers set up almost as many distinct instincts as there are acquired principles of acting.' He ridiculed Reid for his supposed discovery of the root of scepticism in the ideal hypothesis; charging him with innocently mistaking a metaphor for a scientific theory, and for overlooking the leading part which mental association plays, as the cause of those convictions which Reid mistook for infallible constituents of common sense. 'If we consider the general tenor of the writings of these philosophers,' Dr. Priestley said, 'it will appear that they are saying one thing and doing another—talking plausibly about the necessity for admitting axioms as the foundation of all reasoning, but meaning to recommend particular assumptions of their own as axioms—not as being founded on perception of the agreement of ideas, which is the great doctrine of Mr. Locke, and which makes truth to depend upon the necessary nature of things, to be therefore absolute, unchangeable, and everlasting, but merely on some unaccountable instinctive persuasions, depending upon the arbitrary constitution of our nature—which makes all truth be relative to ourselves only, and consequently to be infinitely vague and precarious. This system admits of no final appeal to reason properly considered, which any person might be at liberty to examine and discuss; on the contrary every man is taught to think himself authorised to pronounce dogmatically upon every question, according to his present feeling and persuasion, under the notion of its being something original, instructive, and incontrovertible; although, stoutly analysed, it may appear to be mere prejudice.' Thus, as opposed to the man of straw he set up under the name of Reid, Priestley postulated a materialistic conception of man, as only an organism, the so-called mental and moral power of which was the natural issue of physical structure; his perceptions the effects of their own objects; and on the whole a necessitated system of the universe, which excluded morally responsible agency.

Reid made no reply at the time to this argumentative discharge. In an unpublished letter to Dr. Price he gives a reason for his silence. 'I will not answer Dr. Priestley, he says, 'because he is very lame in abstract reasoning. I have got no light from him. And indeed what light with respect to the powers of the mind can one expect from a man who has not yet learned to distinguish ideas from vibrations, nor motion from sensation, nor simple apprehension from judgment, nor simple ideas from complex ideas, nor necessary truths from contingent truths?'[1] In 1775 Reid writes to Lord Kames:—

'Dr. Priestley in his last book thinks that the power of perception, as much as the other powers that are termed mental, is the natural result of an organic structure such as that of the human brain. Consequently, the whole man becomes extinct at death; and we have no hope of surviving the grave but what is derived from the Christian revelation. I would be glad to know your lordship's opinion, whether, when my brain has lost its original structure, and when some hundred years after, the same materials are again fabricated so curiously as to become an intelligent being—whether, I say, that being will be *me*; or if two or three such beings should be formed out of my brain, whether they will all be *me*, and consequently be all one and the same intelligent being. This seems to me a great mystery; but Dr. Priestley denies all mysteries. . . . I am not surprised

[1] Birkwood MSS.

that your lordship has found little entertainment in a late French writer on human nature. From what I learn the French philosophers are become rank Epicureans. I detest all systems that depreciate human nature. If it be a delusion that there is something in the constitution of man that is venerable and worthy of its author, let me live and die in this delusion rather than have my eyes opened to see my species in a disgusting light. Every good man feels his indignation rise against those who disparage his kindred or country ; why should it not rise against those who disparage his kind ? Were it not that we sometimes see extremes meet, I should think it very strange to see atheists and high-shod divines contending who should most blacken and degenerate human nature. Yet I think the atheist acts the most consistent part of the two ; for surely such views of human nature tend more to promote atheism than to promote religion and virtue.'

This allusion to contemporary French philosophers is almost the only one I find in Reid. The chief works of Condillac appeared before the *Inquiry*, but it does not seem that they, or Diderot and the French Encyclopedists, were known to him. That Kant is not referred to, nor even known by name, is less surprising. This ignorance is characteristic of Reid's home-bred, self-contained philosophy.

Inquiry into our conception of Power or Causation becomes prominent in Reid's letters to Lord Kames throughout 'the seventies,' along with experimental investigations in physics and physiology which show continued interest in natural causes. A letter, written in 1775, contains a curious conjecture with regard to the generation of plants and animals, more speculative than was his habit. He is 'apt to conjecture,' he tells his friend, 'that both plants and animals are at first organised atoms, having all the parts of the animal or plant, but so slender, and folded up in such a manner, as to be reduced to a particle far beyond the reach of our senses, and perhaps as small as the constituent parts of water. The earth, the water, and the air may, for anything I know, be full of such organised atoms.' He then goes on to consider the relation of this hypothesis to the idea of active design in nature, and expresses doubt about the possibility of the atoms being endowed with power to form themselves into an organised body like the human. 'I cannot help thinking that such a work as the Iliad, and much more an animal or vegetable body, must have been made by express design. It seems to me as easy to contrive a machine which should compose a variety of epic poems and tragedies, as to contrive laws of motion by which unthinking particles of matter should coalesce into a variety of organised bodies.' He suggests that the organisation is the issue of constant and uniform divine activity. 'Can we,' he asks, 'show by any good reason that the Almighty finished his work at a stroke, and has continued ever since an inactive spectator? And if His continued operation be necessary, it is no miracle, while it is uniform, and according to fixed laws. Though we should suppose the gravitation of matter to be the immediate operation of the Deity, it would be no miracle while it is constant and uniform; but if it should cease for a moment, only by His withholding His hand, *this* would be a miracle.' This is to say that all natural changes are immediate effects of divine action, proceeding according to natural law or rule.

The suggestion illustrates the bent of Reid's thought in later life. If our common sense of the continuous independent existence of sensible things, and of their manifestation in Perception as directly as states of our own minds are manifested to us when we are conscious of them—if *this* was the factor of the Common Sense that engaged him in New Machar and King's College days, the Power or Causality which all changes in the universe presuppose now becomes prominent, alike in his correspondence and in his books. What is meant by Power, and where is the Power centred that is implied in the changes that are always going on, in ourselves and in our surroundings? Priestley's assumption that matter explains all the phenomena of a human mind; the theory of universal necessity advocated by Kames; and the duties of his Glasgow professorship, all tended to carry his reflections onward from the merely physical to the ethical judgments of the common sense, and so upward from the merely natural to the spiritual interpretation of the universe. 'First that which is natural, then that which is spiritual.'

This runs through his correspondence with Lord Kames. That there is no absolute necessity for men being bad; that their immoral acts are centred and originate in themselves and not in God; that it would be unjust to exact as a duty what it is not in a person's power to do; that what a man does voluntarily or with deliberate intention, it is also in his power not to do; that what is done without his will is not really done by *him* at all; and that real power is moral agency,—these are ultimate judgments, reached 'not by logical reasoning,' but in 'the more trustworthy way of immediate perception and feeling,' to which Reid so often appeals. 'If I could suppose God to make a devil a devil, I cannot suppose that He would condemn him for being a devil,' is in a letter to Lord Kames.[1] The impotence of matter rather than its independence is now insisted on; with the inference that at any rate *it* cannot cause our perceptions, as Priestley supposed.

[1] Birkwood MSS.

He begins to see that power must be referred to mind or spirit alone, and that matter is powerless. 'Efficient causes are not within the sphere of natural philosophy, which is concerned only with the laws or methods according to which Power operates. It exhibits the grand machine of the material world, analysed, as it were, and taken to pieces. It belongs to metaphysics and natural theology to show the Power that continues and gives motion to the whole; according to laws which the naturalist discovers, and perhaps according to laws still more general.'

It was thus that Reid's uneventful life of thought—deep, steady, unobtrusive—was sustained for sixteen years, when he was educating the rising generation in the old class-room at the College; unfolding philosophy in correspondence with a sympathetic friend; contributing essays to the Literary Society which met monthly at the College; and preparing his 'Brief Account' of Aristotle—all until he had reached his seventieth year. On the 19th of May 1780 he wrote to Lord Kames of a change that had occurred the day before:—

'I find myself growing old; and I have no right to plead exemption from the infirmities of that stage of life. For that reason I have made choice of an Assistant in my office. Yesterday the College at my desire made choice of Mr. Archibald Arthur, preacher, to be my assistant and successor. I think I have done good service to the College by this, and procured some leisure to myself, though with reduction of my finances.'

It was Reid's desire, while his faculties were yet vigorous, to devote his strength to further philosophical authorship. During the remaining sixteen years of his life his lectures were delivered to the students by Mr. Arthur, to whom the professorial work in the class-room was transferred. Arthur, then thirty-six years of age, was a native of Renfrewshire, a distinguished alumnus of Glasgow, as it seems from a posthumous volume of his Essays, and a man not unlike Reid in mind and character, but in inferior form; at this time chaplain and librarian of the University, and a member of the Literary Society. After one of Arthur's Sunday services in the College chapel, Reid had whispered to one of his colleagues on the professorial bench—'This is a very sensible fellow, and in my opinion would make a good professor of morals.'[1] He is described by a contemporary as 'a man of unprepossessing exterior, of invincible bashfulness, which continued to clog his manner and impede his exertions during the whole course of his life; but of a thoughtful, grave, silent habit, which led him to a due estimate of what he was individually adapted to.' He survived Reid, as his successor, a little more than a year, when he was followed in the Chair by James Mylne, a strong man unknown in philosophical literature, whose professorial career of forty years made him a familiar figure to generations of Glasgow students.

[1] Professor Richardson's Memoir of Arthur.

CHAPTER VII

PHILOSOPHICAL RETIREMENT: AUTHORSHIP IN OLD AGE

1780—1795

DUGALD STEWART, when illustrating the changes in human memory that are connected with disease and old age, refers thus to Reid:—'One old man I have myself had the good fortune to know, who, after a long, an active, and an honourable life, having begun to feel some of the usual effects of advanced years, has been able to find resources in his own sagacity against most of the inconveniences with which they are commonly attended; and who, by watching his gradual decline with the courage of an indifferent observer, and employing his ingenuity to retard its progress, has converted even the infirmities of old age into a source of philosophical amusement.' For sixteen years Reid had been discharging that part of the duties of a professor which belongs to the class-room: the remaining sixteen years of his life, devoted to original research and authorship, illustrate the words of Stewart. He continued, after the appointment of Arthur, to live as before in the Professors' Court in old Glasgow College—a placid, methodical life, steadily industrious, a sagacious interpreter of nature and of man, still active in the academic senate—with occasional recreation in visits to the country. The year 1780 was saddened by another of those domestic sorrows which formed the chief interruption to the tranquil happiness of his life; for his eldest son, George, died in Newfoundland in February, at the age of twenty-five. Two years later the only remaining son, David, was taken away; after which his daughter, Mrs. Carmichael, alone survived of the nine sons and daughters.

Very soon after he had been released from the public work of the professorship, letters to his cousin, Dr. James Gregory, then an Edinburgh Professor of Medicine, speak of activity in transforming the lectures into the form of philosophical essays for publication. This enterprise was indeed Reid's principal employment for the next eight years. The *Essays* appeared in two instalments, in 1785 and 1788. The first instalment was a matter-of-fact inquiry into the intellectual power of man; the second was a matter-of-fact inquiry into man's moral power: the 'facts' inquired about and appealed to were the invisible ones of which men are conscious, not those that can be seen and touched—above all, the final convictions of which the Common Sense consists. Both instalments appeared in the same decade of last century in which Kant's '*Kritiks*' of Pure and Practical Reason were given to the world.

Reid's *Essays* form, as it were, the inner court of the temple of which the Aberdonian *Inquiry* is the vestibule. But the vestibule is a more finished work of constructive skill than the inner court, for the aged architect appears at last as if embarrassed by accumulated material. The *Essays*, greater in bulk, perhaps less deserve a place among modern philosophical classics than the *Inquiry*, notwithstanding its narrower scope, confined as it is to man's perception of the extended world, as an object-lesson in the method of appeal to the common sense. In the *Essays* an advance is made towards a finally ethical interpretation of man and the universe.

We have no longer the light of letters to Lord Kames in this closing stage of Reid's life; for Kames died in 1782. Reid's retiring modesty deprived him of that large literary intercourse to which his philosophical position might otherwise have led. His correspondence with men eminent in letters or philosophy seems almost confined to Kames, the Gregories, Dugald Stewart, and Dr. Price. I find no trace of correspondence with his Aberdeen friends Campbell and Beattie, whose pursuits had so much in common with his own. But letters to Dr. James Gregory take the place in the 'eighties' which those to Lord Kames took in the 'seventies'; they reveal an old age given to proof-sheets, scientific experiments, and benignant interest in social progress. One dated 'Glasgow College, April 7, 1783,' tells of the *Essays on the Intellectual Powers* in the press:—'I shall be much obliged if you will continue to favour me with your observations; therefore I have put off examining those you have sent until the manuscripts be returned, which I expect about the end of this month, along with Dugald Stewart's observations.' Again he writes in June:—'I cannot get more copied of my papers till next winter, and indeed have not much more ready. This parcel goes to page 658. I believe what you have got before may be one-half of all I intend. The materials of what is not yet ready for the copier are partly discourses read in our Literary Society, partly notes of my lectures. Your judgment of what you have seen flatters me very much, and adds greatly to my own opinion of it; though authors seldom are deficient in a good opinion of their works. I am at a loss to express my obligations to you for the pains you have taken.' He refers in another letter to what he regards as the source of the fashionable agnosticism against which his life was a continued philosophical protest:—'I have often thought of what you propose—to give a History of the Ideal System and what I have to say against it, *by itself*; and I am far from being satisfied that it stands in the most proper place [in the *Essays*]. I have endeavoured to put it in separate chapters [*e.g.* Essay ii. ch. 7-15], whose titles may direct those who have no taste for it to pass over them. I observe that Bayle and others, who at the reformation of Natural Philosophy gave new light, found it necessary to contrast their own discoveries with the Aristotelian notions which then prevailed. We may now wish their works purged of this controversial part; but perhaps it was necessary at the time they wrote, when men's minds were full of the old system, and prepossessed in its favour. What I take to be the genuine Philosophy of the Human Mind is in so low a state, and has so many enemies, that I apprehend those who would make any improvement in it must, for some time at least, build with one hand, and hold a weapon with the other.' So Reid claimed the office of modern reformer of the philosophy of human mind, as Bacon and others had been the reformers of the sciences which interpret external nature.

On 'March 14, 1784,' he mentions the progress of the book:—'I send you now the remainder of what I propose to print with respect to the Intellectual Powers of the Mind. It may perhaps be a year before what relates to the Active Powers be ready; and therefore I think the former might be published by itself, as it is very uncertain whether I shall live to publish the latter. I think the title may be

Essays on the Intellectual Powers of the Human Mind. It will easily divide into eight Essays; but with regard to this, as well as whether the two parts may be published separately, I wish to have your advice and Mr. Stewart's. I apprehend that the Second Part—I mean what relates to the Active Powers—will not be near so large as the First.' On '2nd May 1785' he announces that the *Essays on the Intellectual Powers* are ready for publication, dedicated to Dr. Gregory and to Dugald Stewart:—'I send you enclosed what I propose as the title of my *Essays*, with an Epistle which I hope you and Mr. Stewart will allow me to prefix to them. Whether your name should go first, on account of your doctor's degree, or Mr. Stewart's, I leave you to adjust between yourselves. I know not how to express my obligations to you both, for the aid you have given me.'

The book thus ushered into the world in 1785 treats of those constituents of the common sense that are implied, not only in perception of things through the five senses and memory, but also in imagination and in the experimental sciences that deal with the past, the distant, and the future. One of them contains the rudiments of a criticism of the common sense principles that finally regulate all abstract reasonings, and above all, those that determine our judgments of truths contingent upon Will—human and divine; in all of which what philosophers called 'ideas' seemed to him to spoil the genuine common sense and its inspirations. The fifth Essay deals with the office and relations of our abstract conceptions. Of this Essay Schopenhauer remarks that 'the best and most intelligent exposition of the nature and essence of conceptions which I have been able anywhere to find is in Thomas Reid's

Essays on the Powers of the Human Mind. This was afterwards condemned by Dugald Stewart in his *Philosophy of the Human Mind*. Not to waste paper, I will briefly remark with regard to Stewart, that he belongs to that large class who have obtained an undeserved reputation through favour and friends, and therefore I can only advise that not an hour should be wasted over the scribbling of this shallow writer.'[1] This unworthy criticism of Stewart is far removed from the calm judgment of Reid.

That our perceptions are not related to their objects as effects are related to their causes, is insisted on in the *Essays*, in opposition to Priestley, who treats cognitive acts as the issue of power which belongs to matter. 'Men,' Reid says, 'have been prone to imagine that, as bodies are put in motion by some impulse or impression made upon them by contiguous bodies, so the mind is made to think and perceive by some impression made upon it by contiguous objects. But to say that an object which I see with perfect indifference *makes an impression* upon my mind is not good English. It is evident from the manner in which this phrase is used by modern philosophers that they mean, not barely to express by it my perceiving an object, but to explain the manner of perception. They think that the object perceived acts upon the mind in some way similar to that in which one body acts upon another. The impression upon the mind is conceived to be something wherein the mind is altogether passive. But this is a hypothesis which contradicts the common sense of mankind. When I look upon the wall of my room, the

---

[1] *The World as Will and Idea*, translated by Mr. Haldane and Mr. Kemp, ii. 240. Schopenhauer makes other interesting references to Reid.

wall does not act at all, nor is capable of acting: the perceiving it is an act or operation in me.' In short, the relation between perceptions and their objects is a unique relation, not to be confounded with the causal, the only causality involved being the percipient power that is in me.

Those *Essays* of Reid which treat of the constituents of the common sense that are implied in the Intellect power of man, appeared in the early summer of 1785. In September he informed Dr. Gregory of the opinion of Dr. Price, the most eminent contemporary English metaphysician:—
'I had a letter from Dr. Price lately, thanking me for a copy of the *Essays* I ordered to be presented to him; which he has read, and calls a work of the first value; commends me particularly for treating Dr. Priestley so gently, who, he says, had been unhappily led to use me ill.' He then refers to his own health, which seems to have suffered from the mental strain, now relieved by the issue of his book:—
'As you are so kind as to ask me about my distemper, I think it is almost quite gone, so as to give me no uneasiness. I abstain from fruit and malt liquor, and take a little port wine, mostly noon and night, not above two bottles a week when alone. The more I walk or ride, or even talk or read audibly, I am the better.'

Dr. Beattie writes thus to the Bishop of Chester in October:—

'Has your lordship read Dr. Reid's *Essays on the Intellectual Powers of Man*? Those readers who have been conversant in the modern philosophy of mind, as it appears in the writings of Descartes, Malebranche, Locke, Berkeley, and Hume, will be much entertained with this work, which does great honour to the sagacity and patience of the author. It contains the principles of his *Inquiry*, laid down on a larger scale, and applied to a greater variety of subjects. Dr. Reid treats his opponents and their tenets with a respect and a solemnity that sometimes tempt me to smile. His style is clear and simple ; and his aversion to the word *idea* is so great, that I think he never once uses it in delivering his own opinions. It was not without reason that Stillingfleet took the alarm at Mr. Locke's indiscreet use of that word. It was indeed an *ignis fatuus* that decoyed him in spite of his excellent understanding into a thousand pits and quagmires. Berkeley it bewildered still more. And it reduced David Hume to the condition of a certain old gentleman of whom we read, that—

> Fluttering his pinions vain,
> Plumb down he dropped, ten thousand fathoms deep.'

Whether our power of conceiving is so far a test of possibility, as that what is distinctly conceived must be concluded to be possible, and what cannot be conceived impossible, was a question which interested Reid. It is discussed in the *Essays on the Intellectual Powers*, and also in the draft of a letter to Dr. Price, preserved among the manuscripts at Birkwood ; in which it is argued that our power of conception cannot be a criterion of what is possible. The argument turns much on the meanings of 'conception,' 'possibility,' and 'impossibility.' He thus addresses Dr. Price :—

'I would willingly suggest some subject on which I might have the favour of your thoughts when you have leisure and are disposed for such correspondence. What occurs to my thoughts just now is a metaphysical axiom very generally adopted, and, I think, occasionally adopted by you in your *Review of the Principal Questions in Morals*—That what we distinctly conceive is possible. From this axiom D. Hume infers that it is possible that an universe may start into existence without a cause, and other like extravagancies. The use he makes of it led me to consider it a good many years ago, and I have a strong suspicion that there is some fallacy in it, which has imposed on men's understandings, owing to the ambiguity of the word *conceive*.

'As to the history of this axiom, I suspect it to have taken its rise from what Descartes laid down as the criterion of truth, which he maintained to be clear and distinct conception. *Quidquid clare et distincte concipio esse verum, id est verum.* Cudworth seems to have followed him in this, making the criterion of verity to be clear, self-consistent intelligibility. Those who came after, judging it difficult to maintain that everything is *true* which is clearly conceivable or intelligible, have maintained that everything that can be clearly conceived is at least *possible*. This seemed to be the proper correction of Descartes' maxim, and it has passed from one hand to another without strict examination.

'Whatever is true or false, whatever is possible or impossible, may be expressed by a proposition. Now, what do we mean when we say that we conceive a proposition? I think no more is meant, if we speak properly, than that we understand what is meant by that proposition. If this be so, it must surely be granted that we may understand the meaning of a proposition which expresses what is impossible. He who understands the meaning of this proposition, "Two and two make four," must equally understand the meaning of this other, "Two and two do not make four." Both are equally understood; that is, the conception of both is equally clear; yet the first is necessarily true, and the second impossible.

'Perhaps it will be said, that we may not merely conceive the *meaning* of a proposition, but we may conceive it to be a *true* proposition, and that it is our being able to conceive it to be true that gives us ground to think it possible. In answer to this, I beg you would attend very carefully to the meaning of these words—"Conceiving a proposition to be true." I can put no other meaning upon them but judging it to be true, that is, giving some degree of assent to it. Judgment or assent admits of various degrees, from the slightest suspicion to the most deliberate conviction; from the most modest and diffident assent to the most pertinacious and dogmatical. I conceive there may be inhabitants in the moon; that is, my judgment leans a little that way. I would not use that expression unless the probability, however small, seemed to be on that side of the question.

'If this be the meaning of conceiving a proposition to be true, then the meaning of the axiom will be, that a proposition which appears to us to have any degree of probability, however small, must at least be possible. But the axiom, taken in this sense, is surely false. It would be superfluous to give instances of this to a mathematician.

'If it should be said that conceiving a proposition to be true means, neither barely to understand the meaning of the proposition, nor the giving any degree of assent to it, I would be glad to know what it really does mean. For I am at a loss to know what power of the understanding we mean by the conceiving a proposition to be true, if it is neither simple apprehension, by which we barely understand the meaning of a proposition, nor judgment, by which we assent to the proposition or dissent from it. I know of no power of the understanding intermediate between these two. And if there is none, I think the axiom must be false.

'There are many propositions which, by the faculties God has given us, we perceive to be not only true, but necessarily true; and the contradictions of these must be impossible. So that our knowledge of what is impossible keeps pace with our knowledge of necessary truth.

'By our senses and our memory, by testimony and other means, we have the certain knowledge of many truths which we do not perceive to be necessary; their contraries therefore may be possible for aught we know. But we know that whatever is true, whether necessary or not, is possible. Our knowledge therefore of what is possible keeps pace with our knowledge of truth, whether contingent or necessary. Beyond this, I am afraid our knowledge of what is possible is conjectural. And although we are apt to think everything to be possible which we do not perceive to be impossible, yet in this we may be greatly deceived. You know well, sir, that mathematics affords many instances of impossibilities *in the nature of things*, which no man would have dreamed of or believed, until they were discovered by accurate and subtle reasoning. Perhaps if we were able to reason demonstratively to as great an extent in other subjects as in mathematics, we might discover many things to be impossible which we now take to be possible. We are apt to think it possible that God might have made an universe of sensible and rational creatures, into which neither natural nor moral Evil should ever enter. It may be so for what I know. But how are you certain that this is possible? I can distinctly conceive it, say you; therefore it is possible. I do not admit this argument. May not a man who is a mathematician as distinctly conceive that in the infinite variety of numbers gradually ascending, there is no ratio whatsoever which is not equal to the ratio of some one whole number to some other whole number? Yet the mathematician can demonstrate that there are innumerable ratios which are not equal to the ratio of some one number to another. Many mathematicians, taking it for granted that it was possible to square the circle, have spent their lives in a fruitless pursuit. May not our taking things to be possible, in matters of higher moment, when we can show no good reason that they are so, lead us into unnecessary disputes and vain theories? Ought we to admit that as a just argument in reasoning, or even as a pressing difficulty, which is grounded on the supposition that such a thing is possible, when in reality we have no good evidence of its being possible, and for anything we can show to the contrary, it may be impossible?'

A letter to Dr. Gregory in March 1786 shows the *Essays on the Active or Moral Powers* in the press:—' I am proud of the approbation you express of the *Essays*. I have made some corrections and additions, but such as I hope will not make it necessary to write the book over again. But I wish, if I find health and leisure in summer, to add some Essays to go before that on "Liberty of the Will," in order to give some further elucidation of the principles of morals. I expect your remarks and D. Stewart's on what is in hand. It will be no inconvenience to wait two, three, or even four months.' Two years later, early in 1788, when he was in his seventy-eighth year, the five *Essays on the Active Powers of Man* were published. This was Reid's last appearance as a philosophical author. The eight Essays of 1785, and the five Essays of 1788, all relate to human Power—power immanent or intellectual, and power overtly operative or moral.

In March, a few weeks after the book appeared, Beattie writes to Sir W. Forbes:—

'I have been looking into Dr. Reid's book on *The Active Powers of Man*. It is written with his usual perspicuity and acuteness; is in some parts very entertaining; and to me, who have been obliged to think much on those subjects, is very interesting throughout. The question concerning Liberty and Necessity [of the Will] is very fully discussed, and very ably, and I think nothing more need be said about it. I could have wished that he had given a fuller examination of the passions, and been a little more practical in illustrating the duties of morality. But his manner in all his writings more turned to speculative than to practical philosophy; which may be owing to his having employed himself so much in the study of Locke, Hume, Berkeley, and other theorists; and partly, no doubt, to the habits of study and modes of conversation which were fashionable in this country in his younger days. If I were not personally acquainted with the Doctor, I should conclude from his books that he was rather too warm an admirer of Mr. Hume. He confutes, it is true, some of his opinions; but pays them much more respect than they are entitled to.'

To Beattie's less profound intelligence, indignant sentiment was more acceptable, in defence of fundamental faith, than the calm inquiry and sympathetic criticism of Reid.

The Literary Society which met monthly in the College was occasionally a channel for his thoughts through all the years of the Glasgow professorship, as the more famous 'Wise Club' had been at Aberdeen. Principal Leechman, Black, Moor, Arthur, and Dr. Thomas Hamilton were also members. Some of Reid's contributions before 1788 seem to have been incorporated in the *Essays*. After that he still found vent for his thoughts in papers for the Society, and in letters to Dr. Gregory, chiefly about Power and Causation. Among the most important of those submitted to the Society in his last years, I find 'Some Observations on the Modern System of Materialism,' in which the impotence of matter is maintained; as also in another, entitled 'Miscellaneous Reflections on Priestley's account of Hartley's Theory of the Human Mind.' Then we have 'Observations on the Utopia of Sir Thomas More.' A short essay 'On Power,'[1] in March 1792, was his last metaphysical performance: it sums up his conclusions regarding our conception of causation, as regulated by the Common Sense. 'Observations on the Danger of Political Innovation,' suggested by the Revolution in France, were read in the Society on November 1794.

This last Essay is characteristic. It presses a distinction between two political attitudes that are apt to be confounded—the one speculative, dealing with abstractions, treating the facts of the case and history as irrelevant; the other practical, taking account of the actual conditions, therefore disposed to modify its ideals by a due regard to what has been and now is. The first asks what that organisation of society is, which, abstractly considered, is most favourable to progress: the other cautiously considers how the inherited political organism may with least friction be adapted to the changed conditions of the social evolution. Reid assumes this last as his attitude, arguing that the British Constitution encourages continuous orderly evolution, not sudden revolution, and that this is illustrated in its history since 1688. At first, he had looked with sanguine hope to the French Revolution, but, like Edmund Burke, who shortly before had been Rector of Glasgow University, his hope gave place to fear. It is interesting that it was the *Vindiciæ Gallicæ* of Sir James Mackintosh that had inspired him with the hope; for, according to his daughter,

[1] Birkwood MSS.

Mrs. Carmichael, he was struck with admiration on reading the book, and used often to speak of it as one of the most ingenious essays in political philosophy he had ever met with.

Jeremy Bentham as well as Mackintosh was known to Reid by his writings, as appears in this letter to Dr. Gregory, in September 1788, which refers to Bentham's *Defence of Usury*, published the year before:—

'I am much pleased with the tract you sent me on Usury. I think the reasoning unanswerable, and have long been of the author's opinion, though I suspect that the general principle— that bargains ought to be left to the judgment of the parties, may admit of some exceptions; when the buyers are the many, the poor, the simple, and the sellers few, rich, and cunning. The former may need the aid of the magistrate to prevent their being oppressed by the latter. It seems to be upon this principle that postage, freight, the hire of chairs and coaches, and the price of bread, are regulated in most great towns. But with regard to the loan of money in a commercial state, the exception can have no place—the borrowers and lenders are upon an equal footing, and each may be left to take care of his own interest.'

Three years before his death Reid is found preparing the *Account of the University of Glasgow*, which appeared three years after his death, in the *Statistical Account of Scotland* published by Sir John Sinclair. It was not communicated by him to Sir John, but transmitted by Professor Jardine, in name of the Principal and Professors, at whose request Reid seems to have engaged in this work. It was an anonymous publication, but it has been attributed to him, and it bears internal evidence of his hand. His colleague, Professor Richardson, in his biographical account of Professor Arthur, Reid's successor, published in 1803, mentions that 'the Statistical Account of the University was all written by Dr. Reid, except the statements respecting the business of particular classes.' It shows intelligence then uncommon in Scotland of the mediæval constitution of Universities, and appreciation of the true academical ideal. The life begun at King's College forty years before in projects of University reform, was fitly closed by this account of the great western seat of learning.

Mrs. Reid died early in 1792. His feelings were thus expressed in a letter to Dugald Stewart:—

'By the loss of my bosom friend, with whom I lived fifty-two years, I am brought into a kind of new world, at a time of life when old habits are not easily forgot, or new ones acquired. But every world is God's world, and I am thankful for the comforts He has left me. Mrs. Carmichael has now the care of two deaf old men, and does everything in her power to please them; and both are very sensible of her goodness. I have more health than at my time of life [82] I had any reason to expect. I walk about; entertain myself with reading what I soon forget; I can converse with one person if he articulates distinctly and within ten inches of my left ear; I go to church without hearing a word of what is said. You know I had never any pretensions to vivacity, but I am still free from languor and *ennui*.'

After this sorrow, his daughter, Mrs. Carmichael, lived much in his house in the Professors' Court. She became a widow in the same year, for her husband died a few months after Mrs. Reid. Elizabeth Leslie, daughter of his stepsister Margaret, was also an inmate, and added to the comfort of the closing years. Soon after her father's death Mrs. Carmichael went to live at Aberdeen.

CHAPTER VIII

INSPIRED COMMON SENSE AND CAUSATION: ACTIVE OR MORAL POWER IN MAN

PHILOSOPHICAL recognition of the genuine Common Sense or natural judgment of mankind, especially in two of its factors, which seemed to Reid obscured if not suppressed by dogmatic hypothesis, gave its character to his whole intellectual life. He found, in the first place, that 'all philosophers, from Plato to Mr. Hume, agree in this, that we do not perceive external objects immediately, and that the immediate object of perception must be some image present to the mind.' To rid philosophy of this hypothesis, as a mere prejudice, inconsistent with the absolute trustworthiness, and therefore with the supreme and final rational authority of our natural judgment, was the chief aim of his Aberdonian life—culminating in the *Inquiry* in 1764. He found, in the second place, that 'to confound the notion of agent or efficient cause with that of physical cause has been a common error of philosophers, from the days of Plato to our own'; and it seemed to him as subversive of moral relations in the universe as the other was of physical relations. Accordingly, our conception of Power or Causation chiefly engaged him in Glasgow. This appears in his 'Essays' on moral Power in man; in his correspondence with Kames and Gregory in the last twenty years of his life; as well as in the unpublished fragment on 'Power,' in 1792, which was his last expression of reflective thought. The Philosophy of Perception and the Philosophy of Causation—our common sense of extended reality in our first intercourse with it in the senses, and our common sense conception of 'power' and 'cause' which arises in the presence of the changes amidst which we live and have our being—these were the two poles of Reid's philosophical life. His whole life was a war against two common errors of philosophers regarding these, from the days of Plato to our own, in each of which the seeds of speculative and practical scepticism seemed to lie thickly. If these two fundamental convictions were untrustworthy, then faith in anything must lose its sustaining strength. For our perceptions through the five senses are the first principles of all our reasonings about the actual universe, and our causal judgments are the means of interpreting the realities to which those perceptions only introduce us.

We find ourselves continually in contact and collision with Power that is external to ourselves individually; and we seem, too, to be exerting powers of our own: on the Power latent in the universe, our happiness or misery, our whole destiny, depends. What does all this mean? What is meant by the judgment that all changes in the universe are 'caused'; and what is the origin of this judgment, or of the conception of 'cause' that is involved in it? Are the powers which we recognise in us and around us to be referred only to inanimate things as their centres; or only to living and self-conscious persons; or to both?

Priestley, as an advocate of the claim of matter to account sufficiently for self-conscious life in man, and Kames and Priestley by their universal necessity, confirmed Reid's disposition to inquire further into the nature and origin of the conception of power, and the judgment that every change presupposes what we ambiguously call a cause. His cousin Gregory, too, inquired about causation, and gave the results to the world in an *Essay on the Difference between the Relation of Motive and Action, and that of Cause and Effect in Physics*, which appeared in 1792.

That every change must be caused, Reid regarded as a postulate of which the contradictory was absolutely inconceivable: it was necessarily implied in the common rational sense of Man, and, while incapable of logical proof, was that without which nothing else could be proved. That the things presented to our senses are themselves powerless; that all power is spiritual, referable only to Will; and that this is the common sense implicate of our physical and moral experience of changes, was the proposition which Reid now set himself to justify. Our experience of our own voluntary exertion is the only experience which directs us to the quarter in which power, properly so called, resides. A voluntary agent is our only example of a cause, or of that to which change must be finally referred as its responsible source. We can find no productive power in any inanimate thing. Matter, instead of being the universal cause, is in itself powerless, and can account for nothing. The material universe is virtually an external system of interpretable signs, regulated by non-material power.

Take the following extracts from various letters of Reid's to Gregory, from 1785 onwards,[1] in the unpublished paper on Power:—

'Power to produce an effect supposes power not to produce it; otherwise it is not power but necessity, which is incompatible with power taken in a strict sense. . . . I am not able

[1] See also Reid's *Essays on the Active Powers*, I. 1-6, and *passim*.

to form a conception how power (in the strict sense) can be exerted without will; nor can there be will without some degree of understanding. Therefore nothing can be an efficient cause in the proper sense but an intelligent being [*i.e.* a person]. Hence the only notion we can form of Almighty Power is, that God can do whatever He wills. Matter cannot be the cause of anything: it can only be an instrument in the hands of a real cause. . . . In physics the word cause has another meaning, which, though I think it an improper one, yet is distinct, and therefore may be reasoned upon. When a phenomenon is produced according to a certain law of nature, we call the law [or rule] the *cause* of that phenomenon; and to the laws or rules of nature we accordingly ascribe power or efficiency. The whole business of physics is to discover, by observation and experiment, the laws of nature, and to apply them to the solution of phenomena. Now a law of nature is a purpose or resolution of the Author of nature to act according to a certain rule. There must be a real agent to produce the phenomenon according to the law. A malefactor is not hanged by the law, but by the executioner according to the law.'

Again:—'A cause in the proper and strict sense signifies a *mind* that has power and will to produce the effect. A cause in the physical sense means only something which, by the laws of nature, the effect always follows; as when we say that heat is the cause that turns water into vapour. . . . Between a physical cause and its effect the conjunction must be constant; unless in the case of a miracle. What D. Hume says of causes in general is very just when applied to physical causes—that a constant conjunction with the effect is essential to such causes, and implied in the very conception of them.' Again:—'I wish that the same general name—cause—had not been given to both. They differ *toto genere*. For a physical cause is not an agent. It does not act, but is acted upon. *You* accordingly give them different names; calling the one the agent and not the cause, the other the cause and not the agent. But I think this too bold an innovation in language. Men have been so much accustomed to call the Deity the First Cause of things, that to maintain that He is no cause at all would be too shocking. To say that the world exists *without a cause* would be accounted atheism, in spite of all explanations. . . . The words agent and action are less ambiguous. We say one *body* acts upon another; and in vain would one attempt to abolish this language. To remedy this ambiguity of "cause" and "agent," I say that each of these words has two meanings—a lax or popular and a philosophical. . . . It is remarkable that the philosophical meaning must have been the first, and the popular a corruption introduced by time. . . . Power is first conceived from being conscious of it in ourselves. Conceiving of inanimate beings from what we are conscious of in ourselves, we at first ascribed to them such power as we are conscious of, till experience informs us that inanimate things have not the same powers as we have; but language was formed before this discovery was made. . . . It is a curious question how we come by the cognition of power and cause, so that we ascribe them to things that have no will nor intelligence. I am apt to think that savages, whenever they see motion which they cannot account for, there they suppose a soul. In this period of society language is formed. At length the more acute and speculative few discover that some of the things which the vulgar believe to be animated are inanimate. What use must wise men make of this discovery? Will they affirm that the sun does not shine nor give heat? that the sea never rages nor the winds blow? nor the earth bring forth grass and corn? The wiser part will speak the common language, and suit it to their new notions as well as they can; just as philosophers still say with the vulgar, that the sun "rises" and "sets."'

That morally responsible intending Will is our ultimate conception of Power or Cause, properly so called, is not less the lesson of the Birkwood manuscript 'On Power' of 1792. Thus:—

'Will is necessarily implied in the notion of Power. Volition and what naturally follows upon our volitions, is all that we conceive to be in our own power. What a man never willed can never be imputed to him as his action. A being that has no will can have no power. When we impute powers to dead matter, it must be in some popular or analogical sense, but not in the proper sense. There can be no productive power in an inanimate object. . . . A cause is that which has power to produce an effect. When we ascribe power to things inanimate as causes, we mean nothing more than a constant conjunction by the laws or rules of nature, which experience discovers. Thus we say that the sun has power to retain the planets in their orbits, and that heat has power to melt lead. If the ignorant be led by the ambiguity of the word to conceive power in the sun or in heat to produce the effects attributed to them, this is a vulgar error which philosophy [*i.e.* of common sense] corrects. By what agents these effects are [immediately] produced we know not; but we have good reason to believe that they cannot be produced by inanimate matter.'

Reid also allows that, for anything we can tell, things which have no proper power of their own may be terms in a sequence that is subject to an *absolute* necessity of being the sequence that it is. But however this may be, it transcends our knowledge; we must be satisfied with the common sense conviction of persistent uniformities in fact pervading the universe of change, whether this fact is the result of a divine necessity or of arbitrary divine will. Natural uniformities are presupposed in all our reasoning about our natural surroundings, and without this presupposition things could not be reasoned about or formed into science. All our knowledge of natural events, beyond original perceptions of sense, consists in interpretation of the phenomena of which the senses make us aware. Upon this judgment of the common sense our inductions are all grounded, so that it may be called the inductive principle. Withdraw trust from it and experience becomes blind as a mole. We may *feel* what is present at the moment, but the distant and the future are wholly hid in darkness.

Power or intelligent agency is thus the exclusive characteristic of conscious persons: interpretable order is the characteristic of inanimate things. These are two correlative judgments or inspirations of our natural common sense upon which human reasonings turn. Reid finds when he reflects patiently that he is obliged, by a rational instinct as it were, to recognise himself and other persons as the centres of responsible power, the only sort of power or causality in existence that can be supposed by us; and also to recognise in the impersonal world without, something that in itself is passive and impotent, but which, as a system of interpretable sense signs, may be said metaphorically to form the *language* of nature, of which the natural sciences are (so far) the interpretation. The universe is thus a material order directed by spiritual power, in a measure corresponding to the body and the spirit in man, as man now is. But this larger conception carries us beyond the modest philosophy to which Reid confined himself; although he more than once approached it, perhaps through some unconscious reminiscence of the Berkeleyism of his youth, of which, I think, he failed to see the real drift, as it was unfolded in *Alciphron* and especially in *Siris*.

Yet the following scrap, which I find among unpublished manuscripts of his later life, shows that such thoughts were not quite absent from his mind:—

'The ancient philosophers called God the Soul of the World. This, considered as a figurative expression, is destitute neither of beauty nor of truth. What the soul of man is to his body, that God is to the universe, in several respects; but not in all. There are many respects in which the metaphor fails: (1) The human soul did not make its own body, but God made the world; (2) the human soul is ignorant of the nice texture and mechanism of its body, but God knows the whole mechanism of the universe, because He conceived and made it; (3) the human soul receives much of its information by bodily organs: God's knowledge of all things is immediate and not dependent on bodily organs; (4) our power over our own bodies is limited: the power of God over the universe is unlimited; (5) our bodies are wholly made up of inert and soulless matter: the universe is stored with various orders of living beings and free agents, subject to the Divine Power as their moral governor and capable of paying back the service of rational subjects.'

But the philosophy of the Common Sense, as represented by Reid, did not rise to the conciliation of the natural order of the material with the originative freedom of the spiritual world, in which operating law in outward nature is recognised as immediate divine agency, or a part of a revelation of perfectly reasonable Will in and through a universe of things and persons.

CHAPTER IX

THE END—1796

In the last winter of his life Reid read an interesting discourse on 'Muscular Motion,' in the Literary Society, of which he so long had been a member. After describing articulately the progressive changes in the human muscles which mark the advance of age, and proposing an explanation, he thus concludes his last public discourse:—

'May I be permitted to mention that it was my own experience of some of these effects of old age on the muscular motions that led my thoughts to this explanation, which, as it is owing to the infirmities of age, will, I hope, be treated with the greater indulgence. It is both pleasant and useful to contemplate with gratitude the wisdom and goodness of the Author of our being, in fitting this machine of our body to the various employments and enjoyments of life. The structure is admirable as far as we are permitted to see it in this infancy of our being. And the internal structure which is behind the veil that limits our understanding, and which gives motion to the whole, is, in a manner most wonderful, though unknown to us, made subservient to our volition and efforts. This grand work of nature, like the fruits of the earth, has its maturity, its decay, and its dissolution. Like those also, in all its decay it nourishes a principle within which is to be the seed of a future existence. Were the fruit conscious of this, it would drop into the earth with pleasure, in the hope of a happy Resurrection. This hope, by the mercy of God, is given to all good men. It is the consolation of old age, and more than sufficient to make its infirmities sit light.'

The dissolution of the material organism which for eighty-six years had served the writer of these words was now near. Of his few early philosophical associates, Campbell and Beattie only were alive at the beginning of 1796, and in April of that year Campbell died. Reid followed him six months later. Dugald Stewart, then Professor of Moral Philosophy in Edinburgh, gives the following account of the months before the end :—

'In the summer of 1796, about two years after the death of his wife, he was prevailed on by Dr. Gregory to pass a few weeks at Edinburgh. He was accompanied by Mrs. Carmichael, who lived with him in Dr. Gregory's house, a situation which united under the same roof every advantage of medical care, of tender attachment, and of philosophical intercourse. As Dr. Gregory's professional engagements necessarily interfered with his attentions to his guests, I enjoyed more of Dr. Reid's society than might otherwise have fallen to my share. I had the pleasure, accordingly, of spending some hours with him daily, and of attending him in his walking excursions, which frequently extended to the distance of three or four miles. His faculties (excepting his memory, which was considerably impaired) appeared as vigorous as ever ; and, although his deafness prevented him from taking any share in general conversation, he was still able to enjoy the company of a friend. Mr. Playfair and myself were both witnesses of the acuteness which he displayed on one occasion, in detecting a mistake, by no means obvious, in a manuscript of his kinsman, David Gregory, on the subject of "Prime and Ultimate Ratios." In apparent soundness and activity of body, he resembled more a man of sixty than of eighty-seven. He returned to Glasgow in his usual health and spirits ; and continued for some weeks to devote as formerly a regular portion of his time to the exercise both of body and mind. It appears from a letter of Dr. Cleghorn's to Dr. Gregory, that he was still able to work with his own hands in his garden ; and he was found by Dr. Brown occupied in the solution of an algebraical problem of considerable difficulty, in which, after the labour of a day or two, he at last succeeded.'

It was thus in summer. In September he was attacked by

a violent disorder, and after a severe struggle, attended with repeated strokes of palsy, he passed away on the 7th of October. Thus ended the tranquil life of deep and patient thought, which opened at Strachan and almost spanned the eighteenth century, morally and intellectually the representative of Scottish philosophical restoration under the conditions of the time. His ashes were laid in the College Church burial-ground, within the shadow of the College of which he had so long been the chief ornament, and under a tombstone bearing this inscription :—

'Memoriæ sacrum THOMÆ REID, S.T.D., quondam in Schola Regia Aberdonensi Philosophiæ Professoris; nuper vero in Universitate Glasguensi, ab anno 1764 usque ad annum 1796, Philosophiæ Moralis Professoris; qui in Scientia Mentis Humanæ, ut olim in Philosophia Naturali illustris ille Baconius Verulamius, omnia instauravit; qui ingenii acumine doctrinæque omnigenæ, summam morum gravitatem, simul atque comitatem, adjuvavit; qui obiit 7° October, 1796, annos natus 86. Cujusque ossa cum cineribus ELIZEBETHÆ REID, conjugis carissimæ, triumque filiarum morte prematura abrepturam, sepulchro condita sunt. Hoc Monumentum poni jussit filia piissima, unica superstes, Martha Carmichael.'

After the University of Glasgow had in 1872 exchanged the College in the High Street, with its touching memories, for its new and stately home on the bank of the Kelvin, Reid's remains were carried to the Necropolis which overlooks his old home in the Drygate, and the tombstone was removed to the College on Gilmore Hill.

I find Reid's will, dated 7th May 1792, recorded in the Sheriff-Court Books of Lanarkshire. Dr. and Mrs. Carmichael are executors, with Mr. Leslie and Mr. Rose conjoined. Furniture, books, and papers are left to Mrs. Carmichael, except a few books for the University Library.

THOMAS REID

Of the rest of the property, personal and real—after payment of debts, including £300 to Dr. Carmichael, 'payable in full of my daughter's tocher,' and '£300 to John Sargent, London, cousin-german of the dearest Elizabeth Reid, my wife'—one half is assigned to Mrs. Carmichael, and the other half, in equal portions, to 'my sisters, Mrs. Leslie and Mrs. Rose,' burdened with 'a liferent annuity of £10, to my stepmother, Janet Fraser, widow of Mr. Lewis Reid.' The real property is described as consisting of 'eleven and a half falls of ground, with the whole houses thereon, and the well therein, bounded on the west by William Street, on the north by the property of Dr. Carmichael, on the south by the property of Joseph Crombie, and on the east by the property of John Duguid and Wm. Risk, all in the Barony parish.' This property appears to have been bought about 1780, the year in which Reid ceased to teach in the College.

That this life, much withdrawn from the public eye in the interest of philosophic reflection, was not unappreciated when it ended, is shown by the recognition which immediately followed. On the day after he died the event was thus announced in the *Glasgow Courier*:—

'Thomas Reid, D.D., Professor of Moral Philosophy in the University of Glasgow, died on the seventh day of October. His ingenious and elaborate works, especially his *Inquiry into the Human Mind*, and his *Essays on the Intellectual and the Active Powers of Man*, are noble and lasting monuments of his eminent abilities, his deep penetration, and his extensive learning. By unravelling sceptical perplexities, overturning ill-founded hypotheses, and resting every conclusion on evident principles, he has brought about a memorable revolution in the Philosophy of Human Nature. His character through life was distinguished by an ardent love of truth, and an assiduous pur-

suit of it in various sciences ; by the most amiable simplicity
of manners, gentleness of temper, strength of affection, candour,
and liberality of sentiments, which displayed themselves in the
habitual exercise of all the social virtues ; and by steadiness,
fortitude, and rational piety.'

A few days later a more elaborate study of his character
appeared in the *Courier* :—

' Dr. Reid was unquestionably one of the profoundest
philosophers of the age ; and although some who think it a
proof of weakness to differ from Mr. Hume have slighted the
speculations of Dr. Reid, and undervalued the precision
which he laboured to introduce, his Inquiry into the Senses
will probably be coeval with our language. It is founded on
facts which must continue to interest men while their constitution continues unchanged. In his pursuit of new knowledge
he studied the late improvements in chemistry ; he observed
the great political events which have happened, and contem-
plated that with which the time seems pregnant with the keen
interest of one entering on life. He venerated religion—not the
noisy, contentious systems which lead men to hate and persecute
each other, but the sublime principle which regulates the conduct, by controuling the selfish and animating the benevolent
affections. When vilified by intemperate philosophers [*e.g.*
Priestley], he made no reply, being satisfied with having stated
what he thought the truth ; and when outraged by zealots who
falsely call themselves Christians, he bore the outrage meekly,
using no terms of complaint or reproach. He was to the last
moment free from that morose querulous temper which has
been deemed inseparable from age. Instead of repining at
the prosperity and enjoyments of the young, he delighted in
promoting them ; and after having lost all his own family except
one daughter, he continued to treat children with such conde-
scension and benignity that some very young ones noticed the
peculiar kindness of his eye. His end accorded with the
wisdom and goodness of his life. He used sometimes to say,
" I am ashamed of having lived so long after having ceased to
be useful," though at that very time he was acquiring and communicating useful knowledge. During his last illness, which
was severe, he complained of nothing but the trouble that he

gave his affectionate family, and he looked to the grave as a place not of rest merely but of triumph.'

The affectionate judgment of his contemporaries, in the first days of sorrow, instead of exceeding, fall short of the deliberate judgment of leaders of European thought in a later generation. The rise of his reputation was slow. As there are too many who make themselves appear more wise than they are, it was the more uncommon fault of Reid to appear less a philosopher than he really was. Extreme caution made him suspicious of ingenious conjecture in matter-of-fact inquiry, and perhaps blinded him to the large part which imagination as well as reason has to play in progress. 'It is genius, and not the want of it,' he says, 'that adulterates philosophy, and fills it with error and false theory'; and in the spirit of this warning, as well as by temperament, he was intellectually conservative more than progressive or adventurous.

In outward appearance he was somewhat under the middle size, with a bodily constitution of uncommon strength and tenacity, maintained by a methodically regulated life and habitual serenity of temper. Raeburn's picture, now in Fyvie Castle, for which he sat during his last visit to Edinburgh, expresses the deep and persistent thought, as well as the reposeful and benevolent temper, which gave unity to his long life. Copies of this picture are preserved at Birkwood, in the College of Glasgow, and in the National Portrait Gallery at Edinburgh, as well as in the great window of the Mitchell Hall of Marischal College. There is also an excellent medallion by Tassie, done six years before Reid's death.

After the death of Mrs. Carmichael, in February 1805, all who were descended of the Rev. Lewis Reid of

Strachan, by his wife Margaret Gregory, had passed away. His second wife and widow died at Aberdeen in 1798, like her stepson, in her eighty-seventh year, having survived him about eighteen months. The great-granddaughter of Mrs. Leslie his half-sister, Grace Anna Leslie, now of Birkwood, married Dr. Ross Paterson in 1864. Their youngest daughter has charge of the Reid family papers, to which I owe many facts first published in these pages. A son of his other half-sister, Mrs. Rose, a medical officer in the Indian army, was introduced in 1805 to Sir James Mackintosh, then Recorder of Bombay, by Professor Ogilvie of Aberdeen, as a relative of the advocate of the final philosophical appeal to the Common Sense; and Mackintosh in a letter to Mr. Ogilvie expresses the deep interest with which he saw 'the nephew of Dr. Reid, whose philosophy, like you, I do not embrace, but whose character and talents every cultivator of science must venerate.' Sir James's later judgments of the philosophy, after a more attentive study of its scope, were more favourable.

CHAPTER X

RETROSPECTIVE AND CRITICAL

WE find truth, as Pascal says, not only by logical reasoning but by an act of immediate reason, not to be effaced by all the subtleties of the speculative sceptic, who is thus confounded by the resistance of rational human nature. This is a general expression of Reid's more elaborate reply to sceptical distrust in all human knowledge and belief. That genuine human nature, when awakened into conscious life, is practically irresistible, is what Reid insists on; for no sane man acts in contradiction to the common sense of which he is conscious, although he can speculate sceptically in an abstract way, and may even serve truth in doing so. For this scepticism may amend philosophical systems in which the constituent principles of human nature are not theoretically recognised in their integrity; and it may also stimulate the unphilosophical to a deeper and truer insight of what the natural principles are on which men must proceed in their actions. But the principles themselves are not reached by reasoning: they are the inspiration of God; and it is this divine inspiration that makes experience and reasoning at all possible for men.

That I am an individual self-conscious person, to whom something other than, and independent of, my individual self is presented in my senses—so independent of me individually that it can inform me of the existence of other persons whose conscious life is numerically different from mine; that the free agency of a person is the only sort of power that we are obliged to recognise, persons being revealed as responsible powers in and through our moral nature; and that the powerless things of sense, of which we are immediately percipient in our sense perceptions, are interpretable for purposes of common life and science, inasmuch as their changes must be determined by natural laws, all reasoning being otherwise impossible—*these* I think are the chief 'inspirations' or 'revelations' of the Common Sense on which Reid enlarges. This account of those inspirations is not offered as complete; only as results, more or less fragmentary, reached by the deep and steady reflection of a long life.

Reid's philosophical appeal to the divine inspirations of the common sense, without which nothing can be proved, on behalf of truths which do not admit of direct logical proof, but only of a sort of philosophical justification, has been disparaged as an ignoble retreat from the standpoint of the philosopher, in the interest of popular prejudices and blind authority. It has been spoken of as an appeal from the reasoned judgments of the reflecting minority to the unreasoned opinions of the unreflecting majority, an opening for arbitrary dogmas to enter and crush free inquiry. This is the drift of the criticism of Priestley in last century, and of Ferrier in this, while Kantian critics complain of Reid's lazy arrest of philosophy at the level of ordinary beliefs. Besides this, what Reid claims as 'the chief merit of his philosophy'—that of questioning the common assumption that external things cannot present themselves in our perceptions, but only unauthenticated representations of them—proceeds, according to Priestley, on a misinterpretation of the metaphorical language of philosophers: to refute it is an idle waste of controversial labour, taking figures of speech for serious science.

If 'common sense' in this philosophy means only unintelligent opinion, as opposed to the judgments of thinkers, Reid's response to the sceptic may well be regarded as an arrest of intelligence, — blind dogmatism instead of philosophy. But candid critics interpret words in the meaning intended by those who use them. This appeal to the judgments named those of the common sense, is intended as an appeal to reason itself—reason, that is to say, in its final form in a finite intelligence, whose experience of the universe is incomplete, and working under conditions imposed upon its exercise in intelligent beings who are not omniscient. Reid's Common Sense is the final perception of a being who can know the universe of reality only in part, and is therefore needed by man in that intermediate position in which an absolute beginning or end of things must be to him incomprehensible. It is an appeal to that which must in reason be final, in an intelligence that only partly shares in divine omniscient reason. Although its judgments are not evolved from premises, they are nevertheless what all men, except infants and lunatics, more or less distinctly acknowledge in their individual actions, although they may misconstrue them in their uneducated opinions, or spoil them by indulgence in purely speculative systems. The divine inspiration of the common sense is therefore man's final support, amidst the so-called 'contingencies' of temporal change in himself and his surroundings. A philosophical appeal to it is of practical importance in reference to what, at the human point of view, are contingent truths of moral reasoning: the necessary truths of abstract thought, it has been well said, 'sufficiently guard themselves.'

Accordingly the judgments of the common sense which chiefly interested Reid are what he calls first principles of 'contingent' truths, as distinguished from abstract necessities the opposites of which are self-contradictory or unthinkable. Contingent truths, on the other hand, may be rejected in thought; but those who reject them speculatively must proceed upon them in their actions and reasonings, including even sceptical reasonings. The man whose scepticism involves a practical surrender of the common judgment, that what we call the outward world is independent enough of *his* individual existence to make it a trustworthy medium of intercourse for him with other living persons; and who acts accordingly on the belief that 'other persons' are only conscious states of his own individual mind, would be pronounced a lunatic. Again, the fatalist, who rejects practically the moral judgment that refers the issues of a deliberate voluntary determination to the voluntary or personal agent as its responsible centre, insanely sits still in the midst of danger, and refrains from exerting a power which he denies. And he who refuses to proceed upon the logically undemonstrable postulate of universal natural order, by ceasing to reason about wholly uninterpretable chaos, is inevitably crushed by the Universal Power that he ignores.

It is thus that practical disregard of inspired final reason appears to Reid to be 'destructive at once of the science of the philosopher, the prudence of the man of the world, and the faith of the Christian.' The unjust as well as the just, so far as they live at all, must, he sees, live by faith in what cannot be either proved or disproved by direct demonstration. And if all those final judgments of practical reason were contradicted in daily action, as well as in academic theory, 'piety, patriotism, parental affection, and private virtue would appear as ridiculous as knight-errantry: the pursuits of pleasure, ambition, and avarice must be grounded upon this sort of belief as well as those that are honourable and virtuous.'

On the other hand there are common prejudices which, while they last, are popularly dignified as 'common sense.' Some now universally admitted truths of science at first shocked men, although afterwards found to be in harmony with the general common sense to which philosophy appeals. That we are living on a material ball that revolves in space; that the revolving ball revolves also on its axis; that the sun does not rise and set, but is at rest; the existence of the antipodes; the invisibility of the distances of things—are a few examples. Instead of contradicting the common sense, the common sense, in the light of further experimental evidence, finally imposes them upon us. At any rate *their* contradictories cannot be justified by the universal intellectual paralysis which is the alternative to the rejection of a *genuine* judgment of the common sense. The assertion that the earth is in motion and the sun relatively at rest does not contradict sane human nature: that changes in nature are all wholly chaotic, and therefore wholly uninterpretable, can never become a scientific discovery, because it implies subversion of all science and makes scientific reasoning impossible. The invisibility of the distances of things, rightly understood in the light of its evidence, draws no protest from genuine human nature.

Human nature or final reason protests, on the other hand, when the material world is believed to be so unreal that I cannot by means of it find that there are other human beings. The impotence of all things presented to the senses does not contradict reason in the common sense in the way the impotence, and consequent irresponsibility, of man does.

But Reid, I think, makes too little of the service of philosophical reflection, in quickening into conscious life in the individual the postulates on which human knowledge and conduct finally turn, and in developing their meaning. Such primary assumptions as the real existence of outward things; our own individual personal existence; and the existence of God, are held with very different degrees of intelligence, by the indolent and thoughtless and by those who reflect. Advance in philosophy is advance in interpreting the meaning of each of these three postulates, and of their mutual relations, as seen in an improved conception of what 'matter' means, what 'self' means, and what 'God' means. The common sense or final reason of man is developed in different degrees in different persons, in different places, at different periods of human history, and in the same person at different times in his life. It is not individually independent of evolutionary law; although its genuine constituents are latent in each man and may be made to respond to an adequate appeal. The practical reason of the common sense, while not founded on but presupposed in philosophy, may nevertheless be deepened and enlightened in each man by reflection and criticism. Its final action is therefore far from superseding the philosopher, who has to systematise man's advancing experience of the universe in the light of an idealised common sense, or the common sense in the ideal man, which the philosopher tries to approach more nearly. In this intellectual progress the cruder conceptions of 'matter' and 'self' and 'God,' as well as of the final physical and the moral relations of the three postulated existences, are purified and expanded; but always without disparagement to the primary roots. Improvement of human knowledge, in harmony with the awakened common sense inspirations, is our intellectual ideal.

It may perhaps be said that Reid makes his appeal to the root principles of practical reason—the essential sanity of mankind—only on behalf of what no one seriously calls in question; and moreover that he attributes the scepticism with which he struggled to a speculative theory of philosophers, instead of to facts in nature and in man, which suggest distrust in the 'inspirations' on which human understanding depends, in its lack of omniscience. What need, it may be asked, for a prolonged endeavour to justify belief in the existence of the house in which we live, the planet on which it stands, or the human beings among whom we seem to play our parts? Only insane persons—really insane—can be found to doubt realities like these. Insanity cannot be cured by an elaborate disproof of the 'ideal system'; and as for the sane, such common sense sanities as these are safe enough without this philosophical appeal to human sanity. As regards those beliefs—*si non rogas intelligo*. I know all that I need to know, as long as I am not asked to justify and explain my knowledge, logically or otherwise, and remain contented to enjoy the things that unpractical thinkers vainly try to understand.

That sceptical distrust in our original faculties, and in

Power or Providence that is finally operative in the universe in which we have our being, lies deeper than the 'ideal system' which was Reid's bugbear; and also that it arises mostly in connection with less obtrusive elements in the common sense than our perceptions through the five senses, is in harmony with the gradual development of Reid's own thought which I have tried to trace. For he advanced, as we saw, from reflection upon those 'inspirations' of the common sense that are implied in our physical perceptions, to reflection upon those other data of the common sense that are implied in our perceptions of personal and morally responsible agency. It is in touching and seeing the material world that the common sense is first awakened; and thus the material world is the most obtrusive object in human experience, its perceptions affording the fittest preliminary object-lesson on the office of this final reason in the whole rational economy of man. External perceptions are the beginnings of all reasonings about concrete existence. They are the obvious examples of those original judgments, which are 'the inspiration of the Almighty,' more obvious than the often dormant ones that are moral and spiritual. All the discoveries of our reason are grounded on them. A remarkable deviation from them, arising from a disorder in the constitution, is called *lunacy* by all; as when a man believes that he is made of glass: but when a man suffers himself to be reasoned out of them by metaphysical arguments he would call this *metaphysical lunacy*; which differs from the other species of the distemper in this, that it is not continued, but intermittent. He thus tests reason in its final authority, as distinguished from reason in its innumerable inferential exercises: the authority may be logically vindicated as reasonable, but its judgments are not conclusions originally deduced from premises.

It must also be remembered that the Reidian protest on behalf of a philosophical recognition of the blended judgment and feeling which makes this common reason that is more or less consciously alive in all men, is a protest on behalf of the regulative authority of this reason in its genuine integrity. All philosophical systems, so far, proceed upon and acknowledge its judgments; but, as it seemed to Reid, often only after spoiling them. He made it his particular mission to restore them in their genuine integrity to philosophy as the prime factors of all true theories. In perception does the outward reality actually appear, extended as it really is, without any unextended medium interposed, exactly as the internal reality of a pain or a pleasure appears without a medium, when I am conscious of being pained or pleased? If so, let us then, Reid would say, accept this fact as final, even although we cannot account for it; instead of perverting it by supposing that the external reality is one thing, and the immediately perceived object of which alone we are curious a different thing;—dreaming that this supposed internal object, as its copy, explains our perception of the external object that is imperceptible. Again, according to genuine common sense, the 'self' which I am obliged to presuppose is invisible; my body or my brain is external to *it*, as much so as the sun and moon are; for they are all parts of the material world—all objects of my senses—unlike my proper personality, which is approached only through the inner consciousness, and not at all through perception of the senses. Here, too, Reid protests on behalf of the genuine common sense, and against the scientifically perverted common sense offered to him by Priestley. For the distinctive feature of Reidism is not vague acknowledgment of the common sense, but acknowledgment of it as it is found to be when steadfast reflection is applied to the final mental experience of man.

A modern critic may complain that Reid's point of view is too narrow and special, and his method too matter-of-fact to entitle the result to be called philosophy. It looks unlike philosophy proper, which is concerned with the universe and universals, and is like a special science of human mind, having human mind for its finite object or province, as other special sciences have their limited provinces. For instance, astronomy has the stellar bodies; chemistry, the elementary constitution of bodies; geology, the phenomena in the strata of the earth's crust; and so on. Now the final problem of universal reality, or at least universal reality in ultimate relation to man, is the proper business of the philosopher, who contemplates the all-comprehensive synthesis which sustains or explains each special science, and even the universe of nature and man; while, as human philosophy, it still recognises the inherent infinity that makes realities overleap the special sciences. For philosophy is the supreme speculation, concerned with Matter or outward Nature, Self or Spirit, and God or the final all-determining Power—and of this final inquiry Reid had hardly a conception. Yet we must allow that when Reid's method is called 'inductive,' it is more than inductive in the ordinary meaning of the word induction in the natural sciences. He does not reach the several principles of the common sense by the way of probable generalisation from observed facts; rather as truths which arise out of latency into more or less distinct

THOMAS REID

consciousness, in response to steadfast meditation. They are philosophically recognised 'inspirations,' or 'revelations'—not tentative generalisations; and their justification must not be confounded with the ordinary verification with which we are familiar in sciences of outward nature. The common sense provides material to the philosopher, not ready made, but still not mere issue of empirical generalisation.

How far a philosophy akin to that of Reid admits of philosophical expansion, or of being brought up to date at the end of the nineteenth century, when the fundamental questions of religious thought are at the root of our doubts and perplexities, may be considered on a review of the fortunes of Reid's appeal to the inspirations of final reason in the century which has passed since he died.

CHAPTER XI

REID IN THE NINETEENTH CENTURY: DEVELOPMENT OF THE COMMON SENSE PHILOSOPHY: REID IN FRANCE: REID AND HAMILTON: REID AND SCOTO-HEGELIAN IDEALISM: ETHICAL OR THEISTIC FINAL FAITH

How has Reid's protest of reason in the name of common sense—a protest against sceptical paralysis of human intelligence, physical and moral—fared in the nineteenth century? Has Reid by this protest established what is of lasting value either to human happiness or to philosophical theory? What has modern thought, as developed at the end of the nineteenth century, to say to a Scottish eighteenth century inquiry into human mind that finds its root in a postulated sense of reality, which must be taken as finally authoritative when it is recognised in its genuine integrity? How do faith and doubt now stand finally related, as compared with their relations when Reid opposed Hume? Is there still room for philosophical argument founded on the divine inspirations of the Common Sense, under, for instance, our transformed conception of the universe as an evolution?

Expansion rather than subversion of the philosophy which ultimately argues from the common sense, has, I think, been going on. Matter-of-fact study of human mind, as engaged in perception of the material world, and in the moral exercise of voluntary agency, which with Reid makes this perception of matter, and moral consciousness of free agency its prominent spiritual facts, has now risen to criticism of our conception of the Supreme Power that is finally at work in the universe in which we live and move and have our being. And a less purely academic scepticism than that against which Reid summoned the common sense now confronts us. If Reid's mission was to call attention to our direct mental grasp of outward realities, by exploding a theory which seemed to paralyse that grasp, it would have been his corresponding mission now to justify, in name of the moral and spiritual elements of the common sense, the religious interpretation of the universe, which finds in the facts of matter and man a continuous self-revelation of omnipotent love and mercy—and this in the face of a world which repels our more philanthropic civilisation, by its abundant suffering and sin. Instead of philosophy at war with common sense, common sense is now alleged as at war with the finally moral and religious conception of the universe, which Reid accepted as conclusive under the premises of an old-fashioned natural theology. Now universal natural law is supposed to exclude God, and sentient misery to make theistic faith in the goodness, and therefore trustworthiness, of the Supreme Power an anachronism, which must give place to universal pessimist doubt and despair. How can we rest with trust in those practical principles of human nature to which Reid appealed, when they and we are found in a universe so full of evil as this in which we find ourselves? Are we not navigating the ocean of life in a vessel that is not seaworthy? These are questions now expressed or felt.

For forty years after Reid's death the higher thought of Scotland, represented by its leaders, remained well within the old lines. It was still careful analysis of what is

presented in human consciousness, with a gradual decline
of interest in the metaphysical and moral problems which
Hume's agnostic distrust had introduced even into Reid's
modest treatment of the common sense. Scottish philosophy became a search for natural sequences and co-
existences among phenomena, instead of search for firm
intellectual and moral footing in a universe to which we
are introduced by being percipient of an infinitesimal part
through our five senses. For a quarter of a century
Dugald Stewart was Reid's acknowledged successor, less
original, and even less adventurous, than his master, but un-
recognisable in the ill-tempered criticism of Schopenhauer.
With dignified eloquence, wider intimacy with society than
Reid's, and more learning, he applied inductive methods
to find the laws that determine intellectual character
and the education of the human mind, also to solve
social questions, in graceful language—all which touched
the popular imagination more than his somewhat prosaic
predecessor.

Early in the nineteenth century, Thomas Brown, the young
Edinburgh Professor of Moral Philosophy, and colleague
of Stewart, raised a revolt against Reid and Stewart in
some of their characteristic philosophy. This brilliant
youth, minor poet as well as philosopher, had practised
medicine in Edinburgh before his appointment, in 1810, at
the age of thirty-two, to the chair of Stewart. In medical
practice he had been the colleague of Dr. Gregory, Reid's
cousin, and so long his correspondent. Brown, unlike
Reid, was one of the precocious philosophers. At the
age of twenty he appeared as a critic of the *Zoonomia* of
Darwin, and a few years later as author of an *Inquiry into*

the Relation of Cause and Effect, which contains the essence of the philosophy that was afterwards expanded and applied in his *Lectures*. He died at the age of forty-two, leaving works undistinguished by the deep and patient thought of Reid, and diffuse in style, but abounding in ingenious analysis—an interesting contribution to the logic of physical inquiry, instead of appeals to carefully considered judgments of the Common Sense in Perception and in Causation. Brown recognised instinctive belief in natural constancies of co-existence and sequence among phenomena, and treated associations among mental states as the chief explanation of the phenomena of mind. The originative moral agency of intending and intelligent Will, so prominent latterly in Reid, disappears in Brown. And Brown, like Priestley, disparaged Reid's claim to merit for reversing the philosophical prejudice that 'ideas' are the only objects of human cognition, regarding it as a metaphor mistaken for a dogma. Indeed, the empirical laws of association tend with Brown, as with Priestley, to be the sole ultimate laws of mind : perhaps this tendency was restrained in expression as much by personal respect for Reid and Stewart as by conviction.

After Brown, philosophy in Scotland was for a time dormant—superseded by Combe and phrenology. But contemporaneously, in 'the twenties,' a philosophy more akin to Reid than to Brown made its appearance in England ; although the analogy is not on the surface, and has not, I think, been observed. Coleridge, especially in his *Aids to Reflection*, published in 1825, insists with eloquent emphasis upon the difference between 'the Reason,' which is divine or inspired, and mere 'Understanding,' which generalises the phenomena that emerge in experience : he also presses the distinction between free agency, as implied in morally responsible causation, and the mechanical order of nature with which physical sciences are exclusively concerned. 'The Reason,' to which Coleridge appeals, corresponds in function to 'the Common Sense' of Reid. It is described as fixed and final; as in all its decisions appealing to itself; and as 'much nearer to sense than the understanding,' for it is direct insight of truth, whereas understanding must refer all its judgments to premises. That man, because he is morally responsible, must originate, within his individual personality as their final centre, all acts for which he is responsible, is with Coleridge a postulate, 'the proof of which no man can give to another, yet every man *may* find for himself,' and so see the true meaning of the words power and causality. In short, this postulate is among the inspired revelations of the Common Sense that are contained in our share of Divine Reason. We may speak of understanding as 'human,' with its often discordant generalisations; but there can be no merely 'human' Reason. There neither is nor can be but one and the same Reason; the light without which the individual understanding would be darkness.

The philosophy that carefully measures its conclusions by the Common Sense found its way from Scotland into France early in this century, in arrest of the materialism and scepticism which had taken the place of the spiritual philosophy of Descartes and Pascal. In 1811 Royer Collard, eminent as a philosopher and a statesman, was made Professor of Philosophy in Paris. In that year, when he was preparing his lectures, he accidentally found a copy of Reid's *Inquiry* at a book-stall near the Seine.

He was charmed with its contents, which thereafter inspired his teaching.[1] Through Royer Collard, Reid's philosophy became the dominant philosophy of France, and it still retains an elevating spiritual influence in the national schools.[2] In 1828 Reid's works were translated and discussed by Jouffroy, a leading thinker in his generation, who thus leavened thinking minds among contemporaries. But Victor Cousin was Reid's most eloquent and famous missionary. He had been educated by Royer Collard in Reid's principles. His ardent and comprehensive genius, however, became dissatisfied with what he called a 'sage but timid doctrine,' and treated it as a vigorous but hardly philosophical protest against the sceptic in the name of uncritical common sense. In his enthusiasm, Cousin turned to Germany for 'a philosophy so masculine and brilliant that it could command the attention of Europe.' At first he thought he found in Kant the profound refutation of the sceptic, and the grand constructive philosophy he wanted. But soon Kant's mode of expelling the 'mortal poison' seemed as unsatisfactory as Reid's, and he parted company with him so far as to join first Schelling and then Hegel in an eclectic or all-reconciling system. But in the end the fascination of Hegelian thought abated. There might, after all, be deeper meaning, and more capacity for development, in Reid's appeal than he had supposed. So in his later years Cousin returned to his first love. His *Philosophie Ecossaise*, which appeared in its latest form in 1857, is an eloquent appreciation of Hutcheson, Adam Smith, Reid, and Beattie, with Reid as the chief figure in the centre.

[1] M. Boutroux, in *Revue Française d'Edimbourg*, No. 4.
[2] Reid's philosophy was Renan's 'ideal' in his early life, according to his biographer.

Meantime a formidable intellectual force had appeared in Scotland, in argumentative collision with those Germans by whom Cousin had been fascinated, and also with Cousin's own eclectic assimilation of all philosophies. Sir William Hamilton was warning his contemporaries against the 'masculine and brilliant' Continental philosophy, and energetically recalling them to Reid, by two essays in the *Edinburgh Review*—one in October 1829, destructive of the 'Philosophy of the Unconditioned,' the other in October 1830, constructive, on Reid's 'Philosophy of Perception.' The reconstruction of the philosophy of the Common Sense, contained by implication in these famous essays, was, in 1846, elaborated in commentaries which embrace the literature of philosophy, in Hamilton's *Reid*. The Glasgow professor re-appeared in the company of the most learned of all Scottish philosophers, educated especially by Aristotle and his commentators, by Kant, and by Reid himself, whose modest enterprise was now measured by the profoundest problems and most comprehensive conceptions of ancient and modern speculation. The magnificent intellect of Hamilton raised deep questions among us that lay dormant in Reid.

Hamilton in Scotland is so far in parallel with Cousin in France, that—moving in opposite directions—they both helped to *germanise* the philosophy which makes its last appeal to the common sense. Cousin, dissatisfied with the 'timidity' of Reid, tried to reconcile a philosophy that should comprehend the Infinite with the philosophy that is confined to experience. Hamilton's mission was to clip the wings of the speculative adventurers. This made him put the emphasis on the inadequacy of a human understanding for fully coping with the eternal reality. While he praised

Reid for making the Common Sense in its integrity the necessary criterion of philosophy, he claimed for himself the special credit of distinguishing its necessities as of two sorts—the one a positive power, the other the impotence implied in finite intelligence. Hence human experience rests on a conditioned, or (so far) paralysed intelligence; and if omniscience only can be called 'knowledge,' while to know 'in part,' therefore with involved mysteries, must be called ignorance—it follows that man knows nothing. Ignorance is then the consummation of human philosophy, and its highest attainment is this discovery. 'Our dream of knowledge is a little light rounded with darkness.' 'The highest reach of science and philosophy is the scientific recognition of human ignorance.' 'Doubt is the beginning and the end of all our efforts to know.' 'The last and highest consecration of all true religion is an altar to the unknown and unknowable God.' Man's knowledge of existence must be relative to his limited experience and intelligence.

The missionary of a neglected truth is apt to be one-sided and even paradoxical, and strenuous expression was natural to Hamilton. From his first essay in 1829 to his last in 1855 he sought to show the inconsistency of infinite knowledge with our limited share of inspiration in the Common Sense. Accordingly, the negative and incomplete, or what Bacon calls 'broken' character of man's knowledge, rather than its positive victories, is ever supreme in the *Hamiltonianised* Reid, along with a recast of Reid's account of the Common Sense as involved in perception of the outward things of sense.

The respective offices of Reid and Hamilton might be compared in this aphorism of Pascal—'*La Nature soutient la Raison impuissante.*' Need for the common sense with which human nature is charged, illustrates the impotence of man's unomniscient understanding and limited share of the Divine Reason. Taking those words of Pascal, Reid puts emphasis on '*la nature*'; Hamilton on '*impuissance.*' But both are recognised by each: it is a difference of emphasis. Neither Hamilton nor Mansel excludes the conservative influence of '*la nature,*' taken in its integrity, in the way Mr. Herbert Spencer does, when he rests philosophy only on the strongly emphasised part of Hamiltonian philosophy. In Hamilton the '*raison impuissante*' is insisted on really in order to make room for '*la nature*'; on the ground that the logical understanding, here '*la raison,*' is too impotent to be able to *disprove* the genuine judgments of the Common Sense.

Brown's rebellion against Reid early in the century, in the interest of a universal physical causation or association, has its parallel in Ferrier's revolt, in the middle of the century, against the Hamiltonian Reid, in the interest of abstract metaphysics as opposed to uncriticised common sense. In the name of philosophy he excludes from philosophy all except necessary truths of abstract reason; neglecting, as beneath its regard, the world of change, in which Reid's mixed and practical reason, or Common Sense, had been offered as final guide. The office of philosophy, according to Ferrier, is among the eternal truths, which alone can be absolutely demonstrated, and which relieve philosophy from 'the oversight of popular opinion and the errors of psychological science,' which had been unworthily dignified as the final test of truth. The natural beliefs of mankind, instead of being worshipped as divine, are banished in Ferrier's philosophy, on the ground that their self-contradictoriness is demonstrable: the business of the philosopher, accordingly, is to substitute 'reasonable thinking' for 'common sense.' The *raison impuissante*,' emphasised by Hamilton—the ignorance in which Hamilton revels—is not allowed by Ferrier to be ignorance at all; for 'man cannot be said to be ignorant of self-contradictions that can be knowledge for no mind, human or divine.' Independent or unperceived matter is not merely hid from man's knowledge on account of his *'raison impuissante'*; it is hid from all intelligence, because inconsistent with the *necessarily* mind-dependent essence of Being. Pure reason does not need to be finally supplemented by practical principles of common sense. It is able to shift for itself without this surrender. The conciliation of common sense thinking and philosophy is accomplished by the submission of common sense to universal compulsory reason. Opinion must submit to demonstration, instead of demonstration, intelligible only by the few, having to make way for the undemonstrable dogmas of the unreflecting.

Reid, I suspect, could hardly recognise, in the stuffed figure thus put up by Ferrier to be knocked down, either the 'common sense' in which *he* found the root of a human knowledge of the realities revealed in place and time throughout the long experience of man, or the 'perception' in which things external to the individual mind make their appearance 'in part.' The practical impossibility of disbelieving the existence of other living beings, of discarding memory as wholly delusion, of treating man as irresponsible, and our surroundings as chaotic or wholly uninterpretable, alike for science and in common life—these were alleged constituents of the common sense with which Reid concerned himself. They all lie outside the demonstrations of Ferrier, in which he unfolds his theory in forms of artistic beauty and easy grace, which make him the most picturesque figure in the succession of Scottish philosophers. Yet Brown and Ferrier in the end helped on the expansion of Reid.

Before Ferrier passed away in 1864, a revolution in the conception of the universe was in progress in Britain. The idea of continuous physical evolution of external nature and of man, promulgated biologically by Darwin, and by Mr. Herbert Spencer as the all-comprehensive generalised law of a universe that was supposed to be the outcome of unknowable Power, has become a popular creed within the last forty years. Simultaneously, methods of development akin to Hegel were introduced by Dr. Hutcheson Stirling in his *Secret of Hegel*, and afterwards in Glasgow by Dr. Caird, who adorned Reid's chair for nearly thirty years— methods for making explicit latent Divine Reason as what explains and sustains the universe. Reid's appeal in a practical temper, to the mixed and moral reason in man, as that with which man is inspired—an appeal widened and prolific of deeper questions in Hamilton—was still too cautious to attempt to formulate the mysteries of existence, in fully intelligible principles, which should remove the darkness around the 'little light' with which Reid was satisfied. He would have looked with distrust at the more ambitious intellectual constructions which seemed to be superseding the common sense of human nature, as the human response to the sceptic or agnostic, whose philosophical knowledge turned all knowledge into ignorance at the last. Reid was too human to be satisfied with merely physical generalisations of sequences and co-existences of phenomena, finally unintelligible, and therefore unworthy of trust; and he would have been too cautious to accept a network of abstract intellectual necessities, latent in the universe, as the last and best human account of nature and man as actually found in place and time. To rest satisfied with the evolutionary generalisation he would have regarded as involving the 'common error of philosophers since the days of Plato,' in confounding moral agency with physical causation. Of the magnificent Hegelian constructions he would probably have said, what he says of Samuel Clarke's theological demonstration—'These are the speculations of men of superior genius. But whether they be as solid as they are sublime, or whether they be the wanderings of imagination in a region beyond the limit of human understanding, I am unable to determine.'

The alternatives presented to this generation—either agnostic pessimist despair or universal science in which man is in some sense identified with God—final nescience *versus* final omniscience—ultimate and universal problem of existence taking the place of a Reid's science of human mind— represent the unending struggle between sceptical distrust of the Universal Power, ignorantly worshipped, and reasonable ethical faith in the Universal Power, with consequent hope for men. It is in Scotland a new form of the war with David Hume to which Reid's life was given. It has been going on since Socrates argued with the Sophists at Athens, and since Job justified the morality of Providence among the Eastern emirs. The eighteenth-century question, 'What is Matter?' has risen in the nineteenth to the question, 'What is God?' The inspired Common Sense or Common Reason of Reid seems to be sublimated in universally necessitating dialectical Reason, in this Scoto-German way of resisting the agnostic. To fill the place of the 'unknown and unknowable God' of the Hamiltonian emphasis, human knowledge appears identified and co-extensive with the Divine, in an absolute idealism, presumed to be the only adequate refutation of all subverting doubt. The '*raison impuissante*,' sustained by and culminating in '*la nature*,' or inspired common sense, is exchanged for what looks like a pantheistic necessity that leaves no room for moral agency in man or God, and which scorns the incomplete knowledge that cannot dispense with a faith venture at its root.

Yet Reid, if he were now among us, might find the common sense not superseded but idealised, in the more articulate response of reason in man to the all-pervading active Reason which the later philosopher identifies with his own. That the common sense latent in man is the inspiration of God is an assumption with which he started in his *Inquiry*. 'The inspiration of the Almighty giveth man understanding.' 'The spirit of man is the lamp of the Lord.' So the common sense moral trust in God, or universal moral venture, is at the root of all human life and human knowledge, giving unity and vitality to the whole. It is the 'little light'—a ray from the perfect divine light,—and the universe is interpretable for all human purposes only in and through it. It is that in each of us through which the inspirations in the ideal man, when dormant in individuals, can nevertheless be made to respond, in an ethical or religious common sense of the infinite love and mercy of the all-sustaining Power that is always waiting to be gracious—to respond to the inspirations of Hebrew prophets and Christian apostles.

If 'knowledge' means only what is reached by the logical understanding elaborating materials given by sense; and if the name is denied to the inspirations of the Common Sense, what those inspirations should be called becomes a question about the meaning of a word. God is then 'unknowable' by man, only inasmuch as faith in the perfect reason and goodness of the Universal Power is more than an ordinary scientific generalisation. But if we recognise in the Common Sense, and in its underlying Theistic Faith, that without which all our knowledge must dissolve in ignorance, then the faith must be accepted as in reason the final ground of the knowledge; and therefore as in us the last form of the universal reason, in and through which what is divine in us protests against limitation to an intelligence that becomes paralysed in the absence of this its indispensable factor. If knowledge means omniscient physical science of the universe of reality, then the universe of reality *is* finally unknown and unknowable. But if man *can* live in intelligible relations to what transcends natural science,—call this which enables him so to live, 'knowledge,' 'science,' 'common sense,' 'faith,' 'inspiration,' 'revelation,' 'feeling,' or 'reason,'— it is treasure found for the philosopher.

Can Reid's 'common sense' be sublimated into the universal consciousness of Hegelian dialectic, and does this translation of faith into absolute science constitute the true ideal of Scottish common sense philosophy at the end of the nineteenth century? Is common knowledge, and scientific knowledge in special sciences, only knowledge 'in part,' while the true philosopher may aspire to know even as God knows? Must man thus claim omniscience as the only fit ground of his protest against sceptical nescience?

Or, must his interpretation of the experience through which he is passing be, even in the end, only an inspired faith-venture, instead of the omniscience which elevates the common sense into itself? Rather, must not the supposed omniscience, which is dissatisfied with faith-ventures, because faith is supposed to be blind, be itself only the common sense under another name—but with its intellectual constitution more articulately explicated?

Surely only omniscience and omnipotence can dispense with the moral and religious venture of our inspired common sense and its implied theistic faith, as the root of reason in man—in his intermediate place and office, between perfect knowledge and total ignorance. So understood, Reid's philosophy is *virtually* the philosophy that makes its final appeal to the divine in man, latent in each individual man, in and through whom the universe is gradually interpreted as a revelation of perfect reason or perfect goodness. True philosophy is then the moral and religious venture which accepts and applies the principles of common sense, in the assurance that, in genuine submission to their inspired authority, we cannot finally be put to intellectual or moral confusion. Faith in God is latent even in the perceptions of external sense, in which Reid found the first example of the operation of this inspiration. Alike in the outer world of the senses, and in free or responsible agency in man, filial faith, ethical or theistic, may be justified by reasoning, although it cannot be reached by logic as a direct conclusion from premises. It is our primary postulate, and not an object of logical proof; therefore credible in reason while it is not demonstrable.

In this way a humanised Hegelianism, which seeks to

restore or retain the often dormant faith in the perfectly good God, and thus in the future of man, may even be taken as in line with Reid, under the altered intellectual conditions at the end of the nineteenth century. It virtually appeals at last to moral faith.[1]

Poetry in another way than philosophy expresses and interprets for man the inspired experience that transcends physical science and its logical understanding. And we find in the great poets of the Victorian era an appeal through the imagination to those elements in human nature, to which Reid made argumentative appeal as a philosopher. In this lies Wordsworth's 'healing power.' His 'Intimations of Immortality' express divine inspirations, through which man learns to understand himself and his surroundings—inspirations that, dormant, 'fade into the light of common day,' yet, recovered by reflection, 'in a season of calm weather, though inland far we be, our souls have sight of that immortal sea which brought us hither.' And 'In Memoriam' is Tennyson's protest against the doubting spirit of the age, on behalf of the final and life-determining principles, which underlie creeds, belong to our earliest childhood, and on which the wisest and best have rested with a more or less intelligent consciousness through the ages—God revealed in the ideal man latent in all men. The human office of inspired common sense or ethical reason, final for beings whose 'knowledge' must be intermediate between omniscience and blind ignorance of mere sense and feeling, is its tacit philosophy—

[1] So in the 'Preliminary Notice,' in the new edition of Dr. Stirling's *Secret of Hegel*—last paragraph.

> ' Our wills are *ours*, we know not how,
> Our wills are ours, to make them Thine.
>
> We have but *faith* : we cannot *know* ;
>   For knowledge is of things we see ;
>   And yet we trust it comes from *Thee*,
> A beam in darkness : let it *grow*.
>
> Let knowledge grow from more to more,
>   But more of reverence in us dwell ;
>   That mind and soul, according well,
> May make one music as before,
>
> But vaster.'

Our scientific interpretation of the ever-changing universe at last rests on ethical theistic faith, and the Christian revelation of divine love is responded to by the divine inspiration of God in Man, in the form of the spiritual Common Sense. If this be not so, we cannot rely on the Common Sense, for it then belongs to a morally untrustworthy universe.

Established on this faith, philosophy or theology, in Scotland and throughout the world, awaits the sceptical criticism and the spiritual healing power of the masters of thought in the twentieth century, for its further development, and application to human affairs.

THE END